Hiking
South Dakota's
Black Hills Country

by
Bert and Jane Gildart

FALCON

Falcon Press® Publishing Co., Inc.,
Helena, Montana

A FALCON GUIDE

Falcon Press is continually expanding its list of recreational guidebooks. All books include detailed descriptions, accurate maps, and all the information necessary for enjoyable trips. You can order extra copies of this book and get information and prices for other Falcon guidebooks by writing Falcon Press, P.O. Box 1718, Helena, MT 59624 or calling toll-free 1-800-582-2665. Also, please ask for a free copy of our current catalog. Our e-mail address is: falconbk@ix.netcom.com

©1996 by Falcon Press Publishing Co., Inc.,
Helena and Billings, Montana.

All rights reserved, including the right to reproduce this book or parts thereof in any form, except for inclusion of brief quotations in a review.

Printed in the United States of America.

All black-and-white photos by authors.

Cover photo by Lawrence Parent.

Library of Congress Catologing-in-Publication Data

Gildart, Robert C.
    Hiking South Dakota's Black Hills Country / by Bert and Jane Gildart.
          p. cm.
    "A Falcon guide."--T.P. verso.
    Includes bibliographical references (p.).
    ISBN 1-56044-482-7 (pbk.)
        1. Hiking—South Dakota—Guidebooks.   2. Black Hills (S.D. and Wyo.) —Guidebooks. I. Gildart, Jane. II. Title.
GV199.42.S6G55   1996
917.83'9042—dc20   96-34208
                                          CIP

CAUTION

Outdoor recreational activities are by their very nature potentially hazardous. All participants in such activities must assume the responsibility for their own actions and safety. The information contained in this guidebook cannot replace sound judgment and good decision–making skills, which help reduce risk exposure, nor does the scope of this book allow for disclosure of all the potential hazards and risks involved in such activities.

Learn as much as possible about the outdoor recreational activities in which you participate, prepare for the unexpected, and be cautious. The reward will be a safer and more enjoyable experience.

 Text pages printed on recycled paper.

To Scott, Karen, Angie, Katie, and David.
May the mountains, prairies, and trails always be there for you.

CONTENTS

ACKNOWLEDGMENTS

No book ever gets into print without lots of help. This one is no exception. During the course of our work, we have relied on many people, particularly those associated with the various management agencies of the Black Hills.

From our readers we learned much and, although the list is long, we'd like to mention the following people, who helped us immeasurably: Jerry Hagen, Trail Coordinator for the Bearlodge District in Wyoming; Marianne Mills of Badlands National Park; Jon Corey, Sally Svenson, and Craig Pugsley of Custer State Park; Ron Terry of Wind Cave National Park; Scott E. Spleiss, in the Deerfield area; Steve Baldwin, the director of the Black Hills Natural History Association; Galen Roesler, in the Spearfish area; and Loren Poppert and Rusty Wilder in the Harney Range area.

We also would like to thank fellow FalconGuide writers Will Harmon and Donald W. Pfitzer for use of regional material and information about hiking with children. Last but not least, we thank Randall Green, guidebook editor at Falcon Press Publishing Company, for guiding us as we completed our first hiker's guide.

If we've forgotten anyone, we apologize.

BLACK HILLS COUNTRY LOCATION MAP

MAP LEGEND

Interstate	⬭	River/Creek	〰
US Highway	⬭	Lake	⬭
BIA Highway	⬭	Spring	⌀
State or County Road	(000)	Campground	▲
Forest Road	000	Cabins/Buildings	■
Paved Road	▷	Peak/Elevation	9,782 ft.
Gravel Road	▷	Cliffs	
Unimproved Road	= = = = = = ▷		
Trailhead/Parking	◯ ⓟ	Map Orientation	N
Main Trail(s)	▬▬▬	Scale	0 0.5 1 Miles
Other Trails	- - - - - - -		
Cross Country Trails	- - - - - - - -		

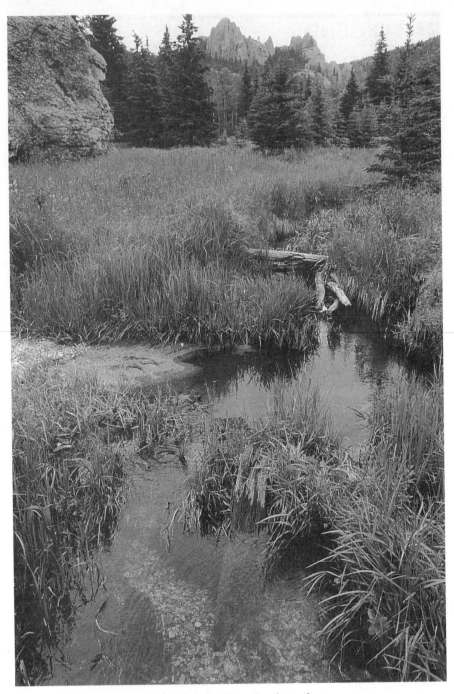

Improvised log crossing along Grizzly Bear Creek trail.

INTRODUCTION

The Black Hills are a hiker's delight. Contained in these 6,000 square miles of unglaciated valleys and hills are more than 500 miles of trails that do great things. For one, they take you to splendid fishing. For another, they weave among incredible scenery sculpted by time in accordance with some of the nation's most provocative geological mandates. What all this distills down to is variety—something for everyone.

This fact is more readily appreciated once you begin to envision the area's immensity and the way in which it has affected travelers through the ages—including Crazy Horse, George Armstrong Custer, and a man named Colonel Dodge, who upon approaching the Black Hills wrote, "The Black Hills country is a true oasis in a wide and dreary desert."

Just what is this Black Hills Country? We think it's a hiker's paradise. The hills' name was ascribed to them by the native people who first lived here and who called them the Paha Sapa, meaning "hills that are black." The hills appeared that way due to the predominance of ponderosa pines. The interplay of light and sun influence the overall effect of blackness produced by these trees.

Geologically, the land represents the easternmost extension of the Rocky Mountain uplift, which covers an elliptical expanse of nearly 6,000 square miles. The Black Hills themselves extend about 120 miles north to south and about 40 to 50 miles east to west. At an elevation of 7,242 feet, Harney Peak is the region's highest mountain. This peak is contained in what geologists refer to as the Central Area. Surrounding it are three rimlike features known as the Limestone Plateau, the Red Valley, and the Hogback Ridge. For ease of visualization, geologists suggest you picture these features in the form of a bird's nest, ringing Harney Peak.

Outside the "nest" are other areas that provide great trekking. For the purposes of this guide, we've included Badlands National Park as well as Devils Tower and the Bearlodge Mountains in Wyoming, which were created by the same forces as the Black Hills. Although divided politically, these areas are contiguous geologically, and we keep them together here.

With such diverse terrain, little wonder some of the region's trails, such as the Centennial and the now-developing George Mickelson, extend (or will soon extend) for more than a hundred miles, while others extend but for a few. We've included a wide range of trails. It's up to you to decide which of the many routes described here you'd like to hike.

USING THIS GUIDE

More than fifty trails wander through the Black Hills, logging 500-plus miles. For hikers faced with this vast country, knowing where to start can be difficult. This guide provides the basic kind of information that will help hikers select trails according to their abilities and interests. We hiked all the trails on public land in Black Hills Country, and give brief descriptions of each geographic region and its primary routes.

The book is divided into sections, one for each of the major geographic regions. Each of these sections begins with an overview, in which we describe the reasons a person would want to hike a trail in that particular area. The aesthetics of the Black Hills' incredible natural history as well as the history of those who have preceded us here through the ages often provide compelling reasons to wander. The overview also offers tips intended to facilitate your outing, something even veteran hikers might appreciate.

Following the overview are hike descriptions for each main trail we covered, beginning with an outline describing the physical characteristics of the trail for quick and easy reference. We give a quick, general description of the route, along with its length. Distances are listed in miles and kilometers.

Each entry also includes a difficulty rating, which can be interpreted as follows: "Easy" trails can be completed without difficulty by hikers of all abilities. Hikes rated "Moderate" will challenge novices. "Moderately strenuous" hikes will tax even experienced hikers, and "strenuous" trails will push the limits of even the most Herculean traveler.

We also make note of the condition of the trail, indicating trail maintenance and traffic. This information was gathered from the managing agencies. In their system, trails receiving "very light" use offer an 80 percent chance of having no encounters with other visitors in a day of traveling. "Light" use indicates an 80 percent probability of meeting one party in a day. "Moderate" traffic indicates an 80 percent chance of meeting three or fewer parties, while "heavy"-use trails offer an 80 percent probability of seeing five or more other groups. This information should be taken into account when planning a trip because trails that receive heavy use are usually muddy in wet weather. Solitude seekers will want to find trails that receive light or very light use.

Following the trail-use notes, we include notes on elevation gain, maximum trail elevation, any topographic maps required for the hike, and directions to the trailhead. After this statistical outline section is, when significant, a mile-by-mile description of landmarks, trail junctions, and gradient changes. We marked trail distances using an instrument called a planimeter, which measures two-dimensional distances on a topographical map. These distances then were corrected for elevation gain or loss and modified where managers had made more precise determinations. The resulting mileages should be looked upon as conservative estimates, however, because they do not always account for small-scale twists and turns or minor ups and downs.

Our interpretive description of each hike also includes geologic and ecological features, fishing opportunities, campsites, and other important information. We've added photographs to this guidebook to give readers a visual preview of some of the prominent features seen along the trail. Where elevation changes are significant, we've also contributed a trail profile chart, which provides a schematic look at the major elevation gains and losses incurred during the trip.

This guide is just that—a guide, not the final word on each trail listed here. Use topographic maps and other resources to round out your regional knowledge, and know your own limits and heed them. You'll then enjoy your travels in beautiful Black Hills Country and have a memorable hiking experience.

CLOTHING AND EQUIPMENT

Comfortable clothes and footwear do more to make a hike pleasant than nearly any other items of equipment. The great variety of hiking and walking situations make it impossible to cover all personal needs in this introduction, but here are a few suggestions for hiker's attire: First, dress in layers. The layer closest to your skin should be a light, inner layer made of material that will wick away moisture from the skin; next should be a warmer, porous layer that can be removed if necessary. Over that wear an outside layer that is wind and/or rain proof. This layering system permits you to regulate your temperature easily by putting on or peeling off layers as weather and exertion dictate. Along with these basics, bring along a good rain poncho or coat as part of your standard backpacking equipment. Rain, snow, sleet, and hail are frequent and unpredictable in the Black Hills.

Each hiker seems to have a different idea about what type of footwear she or he should use. Boots or shoes are a matter of personal preference but, regardless of style and weight, they should be sturdy and supportive. Many people still wear good leather boots for serious hiking, while others prefer lightweight boots with breathable, water-resistant fabrics. The best advice we can give a beginner is to visit a good outfitter or outdoor sports store and try on several styles before finally deciding.

We've included a hiker's checklist in Appendix A to help you as you pack for your Black Hills trip. We've also listed several good books that discuss equipment in Appendix D. Most of these are available in libraries. One of the best is Colin Fletcher's *The Complete Walker III*. Others are available in better sporting goods stores.

PLANNING THE HIKE

Hiking should be fun, even if you hike just for the benefits of physical fitness. To keep it that way, plan hikes that are within your physical ability. Do not attempt long trails or backpacking segments that are more than you can safely accomplish in daylight. Hiking after dark is not only uncomfortable but also dangerous, especially if you are not familiar with the topography and trail conditions. Know the terrain, and study maps before you depart.

Always leave an itinerary with someone before you leave. This should include where you will be hiking, where you will park, your estimated time of completing the trip, and who to contact if necessary. This will lead help to you if by unlucky chance you have a trail accident, or if there is some other kind of emergency.

Hiking and walking seems so simple it lulls the walker into being careless at times. No hike, whether a day hike or a week-long backpack trip, should begin without the basic essentials of a first-aid kit and simple survival items. Think of it like fastening your seat belt before driving to the corner store—just as vital as using it on a 500-mile interstate trip. A first-aid kit is a very personal item, and its contents will depend on each hiker's needs and concerns. However, your kit can be very small and light. For a day hike, it should contain at least adhesive bandages, gauze or gauze compresses, adhesive tape, an Ace or other brand elastic wraparound bandage, aspirin or other pain relievers, antibacterial ointment, moleskin, needles, and scissors (or a pocket knife with scissors). This can all go in a small plastic bag. A first-aid kit for overnight hikes should contain these same things as well as Benadryl or another antihistamine for allergic response, a small packet of meat tenderizer for insect stings, a mild laxative, something to combat diarrhea, and other personal items. A compact snakebite kit that includes an efficient suction device can also be added.

Survival kits can and should be simple and efficient. Carry a compact space blanket or large garbage bag, a whistle, waterproof matches or a reliable cigarette lighter, a compass, a high-energy food bar, 10 to 20 feet of light nylon rope, and a small flashlight. These items are essentials. Keep them with you at all times, especially when on side trips away from your backpack or campsite.

And don't forget to bring enough water. The pristine streams and lakes of the Black Hills are quite refreshing, but may contain a microorganism called *Giardia lamblia*, which causes severe diarrhea and dehydration in humans. The microorganism is spread through the feces of wild mammals—especially by beavers, which inhabit many of the low-elevation stream systems. Any surface water supply is a potential source of this organism, and hikers who drink from lakes and streams take the risk of contracting the painful symptoms associated with this pestiferous microbe. Water can be rendered

4

safe by boiling it for at least 5 minutes or by passing it through a filter system with a mesh no larger than 5 micrometers. Iodine tablets and other purification additives are less reliable.

A FEW MORE WORDS OF CAUTION

WEATHER

Weather in the Black Hills changes frequently and often without warning. Winds sweep off the surrounding plains, and temperatures can drop dramatically. While hiking, we encountered snow in early September, and met cold winds accompanied by drenching rains.

Summer is one of the most pleasant times to hike in the Black Hills, but it can also be one of the most awesome. Lightning storms are frequent and can be nerve-racking as we discovered one day while hiking toward the summit of Harney Peak. Streaks of lightning stabbed the suddenly darkened sky. Only later did we learn how to deal with an electrical storm: Seek

A September snowfall atop Crow Peak.

shelter away from open ground or exposed ridges. Even dropping a few yards off a ridgetop will reduce your risk. In a forest, stay away from single, tall trees; look for a cluster of smaller trees instead. Avoid gullies or small basins with water in the bottom, and find a low spot free of standing water. Stay out of shallow caves, crevasses, or overhangs (numerous in the Black Hills, and inviting). Ground discharges may leap across the openings. Dry, deep caves offer better protection, but do not touch the walls.

Whether you are in open country or in a shelter during a lightning storm, assume a low crouch with only your feet touching the ground. Put a sleeping pad or pack—make sure it does not have a metal frame or metal components—beneath your feet for added insulation against shock. Do not huddle together; members of a group should stay at least 30 feet apart. Then, if someone is hit, the others can give first aid. In a tent, get in the crouch position in your sleeping bag and keep your feet on a sleeping pad.

Watch for signs of an imminent lightning strike: hair standing on end; an itchy feeling one hiker described as "bugs crawling all over your skin"; an acrid, "hot metal" smell; and buzzing or crackling noises in the air. Tuck into a crouch immediately if any of these signs are present.

If someone in your group is hit by lightning, be prepared to give CPR and first aid for burns and shock. Many victims survive, even from direct hits, especially if help is nearby and CPR is continued. Check the person's breathing and pulse and look for burns or other injuries. There is no danger of electrocution or shock from touching someone who has been struck by lightning.

Hypothermia is another risk in the Black Hills, even in summer, since there are times when the factors contributing to body heat loss are present. Cold rains frequently drench the mountains, and it sometimes hails and even snows. Temperatures need not be below freezing for hypothermia to be a threat. Most cases occur when temperatures range between 40 and 50 degrees Fahrenheit, often coupled with windy and wet conditions—the precise conditions often found during summer in the Black Hills, particularly August and September.

People who are inappropriately attired and get wet in such inclement weather have set themselves up for hypothermia. Shivering marks the first stage. In advance stages, shivering stops, but only because the body is too weak to keep it up. This stage may be accompanied by slurred speech, clumsiness with the hands, and impaired judgment.

At the first sign of hypothermia, stop and change clothes— get the victim out of the wet stuff. In more acute conditions, victims should be placed in a sleeping bag with people lying, skin to skin, on either side. Feed conscious victims something warm and sweet, such as hot chocolate—not alcohol. Because acute hypothermia can lead to death, seek medical help.

Custer State Park hosts one of the nation's largest free-roaming herds of bison. Remain alert!

WILDLIFE

Nature runs wild in the Black Hills, and hikers may face risks from wildlife or wild insects. However, unlike other places, bears are not a problem here. No bears remain in the Black Hills, which once provided prime habitat. The last reported sighting of a bear was vague, and dates from the late 1980s. Mosquitoes, also a bane in other places, are few. But a few mountain lions make the Black Hills their home. Today, lions are protected in South Dakota and can be found in sparsely populated areas, including the pine forests of the Black Hills to the breaks of the Missouri River.

Lion attacks are rare—in truth, you will be fortunate to catch even a brief glimpse of one of these creatures. If you encounter a lion, remain calm. Back away slowly, taking care to make yourself seem as large as possible, and do not run.

A more likely animal encounter in Black Hills Country is with bison. Loose bison often are encountered by hikers in Badlands National Park, Custer State Park, and Wind Cave National Park. Always be aware of the possibility of such encounters. If you do meet up with bison, do not panic. Quietly move away.

TICKS

Close encounters of the more personal kind may come as hikers find themselves carrying ticks. Though the incident of Lyme disease in the Black Hills is small, ticks are numerous here. Contracting diseases associated with ticks, is, therefore, a distinct possibility. Deer ticks can appear any time of year if the temperature is above 50 degrees F, even in January and February. If they attach to the skin, they begin to feed.

To a tick, blood has the consistency of Jell-O, which it must thin. To do so, ticks inject saliva and may simultaneously inject a disease-carrying bacteria. Lyme disease, Rocky Mountain Spotted Fever, or the newly diagnosed human granulocytic ehrlichia infection may result. General symptoms of these diseases include fever with shaking chills and severe muscle pain. Lyme disease also produces a rash on the palms of the hands and soles of the feet, which later spreads to the whole body.

The best way to prevent tick-borne disease is to prevent ticks from latching to the skin. Wear long pants and tuck them into boots or bind bottoms with a rubber band. Wear long-sleeved shirts. Consider using a pesticide containing deet, which you should apply to skin and clothing. At the end of the day, conduct a tick search of your body and clothing.

If you find one, don't panic. The process of transmitting the disease takes hours. To remove a loose tick, flick it off with a fingernail. If the tick is firmly imbedded, encourage it to disengage by holding a hot but extinguished matchhead to its back. If the tick does not let go, use tweezers to pinch a small area around the tick's mouth and pull it out. Try not to squeeze the tick's body, since this increases the risk of infection. Finally, clean the wound with an antiseptic.

SNAKES

Rattlesnakes are common in the Black Hills, particularly around prairie dog communities. Though hikers should always remain alert, given their druthers, rattlesnakes will always retreat at the approach of humans. If you've never heard a rattlesnake rattle, don't worry. You'll recognize it. The sound is unmistakable.

Rattlesnakes strike in self defense, and though every few years someone in the Black Hills seems to get bitten, no one has ever died. Nationwide, fifteen to twenty thousand people are bitten each year; only six to ten of these die. Snake venom is relatively slow-acting, allowing victims a chance to acquire medical attention. In 20 percent of snakebite cases, no venom was injected.

Learning to avoid snakes and their bites is relatively simple: Watch where you step or sit down to rest. Wear high leather boots and long pants in snake habitat. Avoid hiking at night. Snakes generally hole up by day, then bask on sun-warmed rocks or sand when temperatures cool in the evening. Snakes generally hunt at night, too, so it is best to sleep in tents with sewn-in floors and zippered doors.

Before proceeding into snake country, bone up on first-aid treatment. Commercial snake-venom extractors are useful if used within the first 3 minutes. Victims—if alone—should walk slowly to the trailhead and seek immediate medical attention. Try to remain calm. If accompanying a snake-bite victim, anticipate and treat for shock as needed.

POISON IVY

Poison ivy abounds in the Black Hills, though the male half of this book-writing team, who is particularly susceptible to the ivy's ill effects, has never incurred the rash in the Black Hills despite much off-trail hiking. Hikers easily can learn to identify ivy and avoid plants that have shiny foliage of three leaves. Remember the saying, "Leaves of three, let it be."

Black Hills vines of poison ivy sometimes reach shoulder height, particularly along streams such as French Creek in Custer State Park and Beaver Creek in Wind Cave National Park. In fall, the plant is particularly deceptive, since its leaves turn a beautiful orange and the plant produces a white berry, somewhat reminiscent of snowberry.

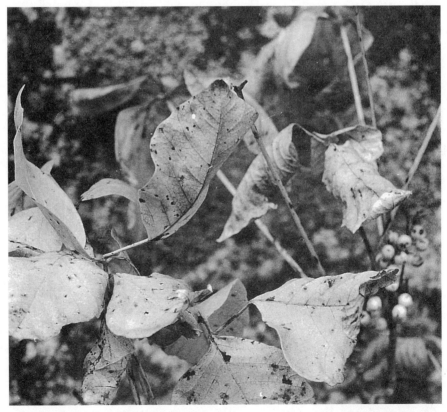

Poison ivy in fall. Note the white berries that may be confused for snow berry. Maintain a wary eye.

Though many hikers prefer shorts, because of poison ivy we recommend that you wear long pants. Trails are sometimes narrow and, under those circumstances, skin exposure is almost certain. Use care when selecting "cat holes" to relieve yourself. Ivy-induced rashes on the genitals can be particularly troublesome and may require medical attention.

If you suspect you have rubbed against poison ivy, wash the area immediately with water from a canteen or from a nearby stream. Washing within the first 10 minutes can often prevent irritation. Ideally, you should place suspect clothing in a plastic bag until it can be thoroughly washed either in a stream or (best) by machine. If a rash appears, apply calamine lotion. Persistent rashes may require something stronger, such as a salve containing cortisone. Extreme cases may require a cortisone injection.

TRAIL ETIQUETTE

Few things are more irritating or distasteful than finding aluminum cans, candy wrappers, and other litter along the trail. "Pack it in, pack it out" should be the working motto of every hiker. This is true for short day hikes as much as for wilderness backpack trips. Get in the habit of taking an extra

Mountain bikes are permitted along many Black Hills trails (such as the Grace Collidge Trail), except those in national parks and wilderness areas. Bikers are asked to maintain controlled speeds and remain on the lookout for those who may be proceeding at a slower pace.

garbage bag on hikes just to pick up litter left by unthinking people on the trail. A clean trail is less inviting to those who litter.

Modern, lightweight camp stoves and lanterns eliminate the need for campfires and stone fire rings. Backpack stoves are ideal for wilderness camping or for brewing up a hot cup of coffee or bowl of soup. Open fires are prohibited in most Black Hills areas, further contributing to a philosophy of taking out what you've packed in.

More basic trail etiquette: Much of the Black Hills is a "multiple use area," meaning that ranchers and their livestock share the fields and woods. Hikers often encounter cattle gates, which should be left—open or closed— as they are found. Multiple use also means that hikers will share the trail with mountain bikers and horse users. Trail etiquette requires that bikers yield to hikers, and that bikers and hikers yield to stock and riders. If stock is encountered on the trail, hikers should move quietly to the lower side of the trail to let the stock pass. Horses are sometimes spooked by unseen sources, so make your presence known.

Trail etiquette also confers the responsibility to care for the environment and respect the rights of others.

HIKING WITH CHILDREN

With the birth of a child, some new parents might think their hiking and backpacking days are over, at least until Junior is old enough to walk several miles and carry a pack. But parents who forego hiking trips during a child's formative years are missing out on some of the most rewarding and memorable experiences to be enjoyed as a family. The kids also will miss a tremendous learning experience in which they will gain confidence and a growing awareness of the world around them.

Kids can enjoy the backcountry as much as their parents, but they see the world from a different perspective. It's the little things adults barely notice that are so special to children: bugs scampering across the trail, spider webs dripping with morning dew, lizards doing push-ups on a trailside boulder, rocks splashing into a lake, sticks running the rapids of a mountain stream, animal tracks in the sand. These are but a few of the natural wonders kids will enjoy while hiking backcountry trails.

To make the trip fun for the kids, let the young ones set the pace. Until they get older and are able to keep up with their parents, forget about that 30-mile trek to your favorite backcountry campsite. Instead, plan a destination that is only a mile or two from the trailhead. Kids tire quickly and become easily sidetracked, so don't be surprised if you don't make it to your end point. Plan alternative campsites en route to your intended destination.

Help children enjoy the hike and learn about what they see by pointing out special things along the trail. Help them to anticipate what is around the next bend—perhaps a waterfall, or a pond filled with wriggling tadpoles.

Make the hike fun and interesting, and kids will keep going.

Careful planning that stresses safety will help make your outing an enjoyable one. Young skin is very sensitive to the sun, so always carry a strong sunscreen and apply it to your kids before and during your hike. A good bug repellent, preferably a natural product, should be a standard part of the first-aid kit. Consider bringing a product that helps take the itch and sting out of bug bites. A hat helps keep the sun out of sensitive young eyes, and rain gear is important. Kids seem to have less tolerance to cold than adults, so carry ample clothing.

Parents with young children must carry plenty of diapers—and pack them out when they leave. Some children can get wet at night, so extra sleeping clothes are a must. A waterproof pad between the child and the sleeping bag should keep the bag dry. This is vital if you intend to stay out more than one night.

Parents with very young children can find an alternative to baby food in jars to alleviate extra weight. Bring lightweight and inexpensive dry baby foods, to which you just add water.

Allow older children who are able to walk a mile or two to carry their own packs. Some kids will want to bring favorite toys or books along. By carrying these special things themselves, they learn at an early age the advantages of packing light.

Kids may become bored more easily once you arrive in camp, so you may need to put in a little extra effort to keep them occupied. Imaginative games and special foods they don't see at home can make the camping trip a new

Needle and spire formations dominate the sky line.

and fun experience for kids and parents alike. Children learn from their parents by example. Hiking and camping trips are excellent opportunities to teach young ones to tread lightly and minimize their imprint upon the environment.

There are many good camping and hiking areas in the Black Hills where children can experience the fun of seeing a beautiful flower, butterfly, babbling brook, or bluebird bringing food to its young. Seeing a deer bounding away in a woodland setting can be very exciting for a child—or a parent. Many units within the Black Hills have excellent nature trails ideal for beginning hikes. Interpretive programs are conducted by well-trained park naturalists and program specialists. Some units also have backpacking, camping, and hiking programs that teach techniques. These hands-on programs teach beginners how to camp and hike, and how to do it with minimum impact on natural areas. Many of the hikes that follow are suitable for family day hikes or backpacks.

To recap, important considerations to keep in mind hiking with children are careful planning, stress safety, and making the trip fun and interesting. There may be extra hassles involved with family hiking trips, but the dividends are immeasurable. Parents will gain a rejuvenated perspective of nature, seen through the eyes of a child. This will reward them each time they venture out on the trail.

FINAL NOTES

Some general information for hikers in the Black Hills:

South Dakota fishing licenses are required for all lakes and streams. A one-day license costs $6.75; a five-day license costs $14.75.

Custer State Park holds an annual Buffalo Round-Up, usually the last weekend of September. This event is open to the public and is an exciting time for all. The buffalo corrals are located along the Wildlife Loop Road and visitors can watch the bison being driven to the corrals. From elevated platforms, visitors can then see how the bison are culled and inoculated. The Custer State Park annual Arts Festival is held on the same weekend as the Buffalo Round-Up. Local artists and artisans are featured, as are bands and singing. A great chili cook-off ends the affair.

Mount Rushmore is the most famous attraction of the Black Hills area, but be sure to include a visit to the memorial (still being carved) to Crazy Horse, located between Hill City and Custer. We suggest driving as many of the scenic roads of the Black Hills as you can. This will give you a better feel for the whole area and help you pinpoint trails that interest you.

And one last note from the authors: Covering every trail in the Black Hills was not our goal. Many trails cross private lands, and we did not hike any of those. We chose to write up hikes on public land, and include only those that we felt gave the best views of each area. We apologize if we've left out your favorite trail or hike. At the same time, we welcome any suggestions or corrections readers might have to offer. Please feel free to write us c/o Falcon Press Publishing Company and share your thoughts.

BEARLODGE MOUNTAINS

OVERVIEW

The Bearlodge Mountains in the extreme northeast portion of Wyoming make up the northwest section of the Black Hills. The range is just beginning to establish its reputation as home to premier hiking trails. Trails in the area now total 56 miles, including many recently developed routes—some created as recently as 1996. How fortunate we are to have these trails, new and old, which wander through significant segments of natural and historical time! "The Bearlodge Mountains are unique," says Jerry Hagen, coordinator for the Bearlodge trails, "since they are a mosaic of eastern hardwoods and western coniferous forest." Hikers here will pass astonishing vistas.

The Bearlodge range has hosted some intriguing historic events. For long periods, the area was home to Native Americans, as evidenced by the thousands of artifacts left over as many years at Vore Buffalo Jump, 12 miles east of Sundance, Wyoming. Archaeologists believe native peoples drove more than twenty thousand animals over the jump over time. Not surprisingly, the Bearlodge Mountains served as the backdrop for Native American sun dance ceremonies—the events later provided the name for the nearby town of Sundance, Wyoming, long before the notorious "Sundance Kid" served time in the town's jail.

In 1874 the area surrounding the Bearlodge Mountains hosted the Custer Expedition to the Black Hills. U.S. Army General George Armstrong Custer was searching for fortification sites to protect local settlers when he climbed high on Inyan Kara (6,368 feet), a mountain the Indians considered sacred, visible from many Bearlodge trails. One of Custer's men, a Colonel Ludlow, inscribed the name G. A. Custer and the date—"74"—on a rock wall on the peak. Today, the remains of this etching can be found by those willing to make the proper inquiries and the rigorous climb.

Wagon ruts from the Custer Expedition are still visible in the fields and valleys of the Bearlodge area, as are other trails of early settlers. Following the Custer Expedition, miners and homesteaders began making their way into the mountains here. In 1881 the Ogdens settled in what is now Ogden Canyon, followed by prospector Emil Reuter. Reuter so loved the area that he remained here until his death some thirty-two years after he arrived. Today his grave may be seen along Ogden Canyon Road.

Area ranchers also used the settlers' trails, driving their cattle to water holes deep in the hills. They were followed later by firefighters, who created paths of their own and reinforced already existing trails. Out of these paths, Forest Service district managers created a trail network, which they categorized into three systems: The **Sundance System** comprises 50.3 miles (80.9 km) of trails; the **Carson Draw System** includes 6 trail miles (9.6 km); and the **Cook Lake/Cliff Swallow System** covers 4.5 miles (7.2 km). For greater access, each of the systems has been located near a Forest Service campground.

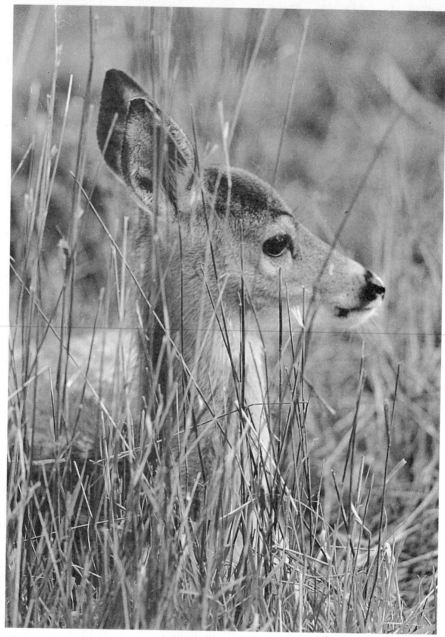

Those who walk quietly are often rewarded with sightings such as this fawn in the grasslands that flank the Bearlodge Mountains.

BEARLODGE MOUNTAINS

To Hulett, WY

Alva

To
Aladdin, WY,
Belle Fourche, SD,
SD (34)

(24)

Bearlodge
Campground

832

Cook Lake
and
Cliff Swallow
Trails

Cook
Lake
CG

843

To (90)

To Hulett, WY

842

849

843

Sundance Trails

N

Warren Peak
Lookout

Sundance Campground

Reuter Springs Trail

0   1   2   3

To Spearfish, SD

Miles

838

(123)

Carson Draw
Trail

Reuter
Campground

To Devils Tower

(14)

Sundance

To
Moorcroft,
Gillette

(90)

(585)

To Four Corners

General Description:	A level lakeshore hike and a longer, moderately difficult path for those interested in natural history.
Length:	1 mile around Cook Lake; 3.5-mile (5.6-km) Cliff Swallow Trail.
Difficulty:	Varies from easy to moderate.
Trail maintenance:	Yearly.
Traffic:	Light to moderate.
Elevation gain:	500 feet.
Highest elevation:	5,100 feet.
Maps:	Free trail brochure from the Forest Service office in Sundance; Black Hills National Forest map.

Cliff Swallow

Finding the trailheads: Both trails are accessed from Cook Lake, 20 miles (32 km) north of Sundance. Find the Forest Service office on U.S. Highway 14 (Cleveland Street) near the east end of Sundance. From the office, proceed 2.9 miles (4.6 km) west on US 14 to Forest Road 838 north. Follow FR 838 for 2.6 miles (4.1 km) to Reuter Campground, which serves as a nice base.

From the campground, go north on FR 838 to Forest Road 843. Take FR 843 north to Forest Road 842, and follow this road into the Cook Lake area and campground. Access the Cook Lake Trail at any point around the lake. Trailheads for the Cliff Swallow Trail are located on the north side of the lake and depart from both the campground and the road. These spur trails quickly merge with the trail proper.

    0.0   Cliff Swallow trailhead.
    2.5   Trail crests.
    3.5   Loop completed.

The hikes: The Cook Lake Trail is self-explanatory, following a level route around the shore of Cook Lake. The lake is stocked with brown and rainbow trout; anglers will need a Wyoming fishing license.

The Cliff Swallow Trail is intended for recreational hikers with an inter-

COOK LAKE–CLIFF SWALLOW TRAILS

est in natural history. If hikers take the loop hike going counterclockwise, the trail begins by paralleling Beaver Creek. Bur oak, aspen, and birch line the trail, while bluffs filled with cliff swallow nesting holes rise on the east side of the stream. Above the bluffs, turkey vultures ride the thermals. In fall, shrubs at trailside adorn the route with clusters of red berries. The area serves as prime deer habitat.

The trail is well marked with brown signs depicting cliff swallows. Along the way, beaver dams impound the nearby stream, adding considerable interest to the outing. Hikers should search the stream for water ouzels, also known as "dippers" because of their tendency to perch on a rock and dip up and down into the water as they peer into the depths for insects.

Two miles from the trailhead, the path begins to wind uphill and away from the creek. The trail ascends a series of switchbacks, none of which is particularly strenuous. The trail crests about 0.5 mile from the creek, providing excellent views of the cliffs that serve as a seasonal residence for cliff swallows.

2   CARSON DRAW TRAILS

General description:	Woods and canyon trails designed for four-season use, offering solitude in the Wyoming Black Hills.
Length:	6-mile (9.6-km) trail system.
Difficulty:	Easy to moderate.
Trail maintenance:	Yearly.
Traffic:	Moderate.
Elevation gain:	2,200 feet.
Highest elevation:	5,700 feet.
Maps:	Free trail map available at the Sundance Forest Service office; Black Hills National Forest map.

Carson Draw

Finding the trailhead: From the Forest Service office on U.S. Highway 14 (Cleveland Street) near the east end of Sundance, proceed 2.9 miles (4.6 km) west on US 14 to Forest Road 838 north. Follow the road 2.6 miles (4.1 km) to Reuter Campground, where the trail system begins.

CARSON DRAW TRAILS

0.0	Trailhead.
1.0	Loop option encountered.
2.5	Carson Draw to Carson Cut-across option.
4.0	Trailhead after loop.

The hikes: The Carson Draw Trails primarily have been used by cross-country skiers in the past, but these trails offer backwoods treks of great beauty and solitude year-round. Hikers and bikers can make a loop hike within the trail system or go on a series of one-way hikes. You may also link up to the Sundance Trail System. Be alert for the presence of horse riders, who also use these non-motorized trails.

The system's main trail departs from the campground and heads southwest before swinging northwest. The path winds through prime habitat for elk, deer, and songbirds in stands of ponderosa pine, oak, and aspen. After about 1 mile, hikers will encounter a loop trail, which lies in the center of the 6 miles of trail here. By hiking north (counterclockwise) on the loop, you can circle around and return to your starting point. Another option is to branch off the loop after almost 1 mile and head north to the Carson Cut-across, which connects with Reuter Springs Trail. Hikers with a good sense of direction (or a compass) can create their own circuits here

---

3   SUNDANCE TRAIL SYSTEM

General description:	Loops among the newest trails in the Bearlodge Mountains, extending a total of 50.3 miles (80.9 km).
Length:	Loop 1, 13 miles (20.9 km); Loop 2, 9.2 miles (14.8 km).
Difficulty:	Easy to moderately difficult.
Trail maintenance:	Yearly.
Traffic:	Light to moderate.
Elevation gain:	As much as 1,600 feet.
Highest elevation:	6,400 feet.
Maps:	Free trail map from the Sundance Forest Service office; Black Hills National Forest map.

Sundance Loop One

SUNDANCE TRAIL SYSTEM
REUTER SPRINGS TRAIL

Finding the trailheads: Suggested access is from Sundance Campground and trailhead. From the Forest Service office in Sundance, go 0.3 mile east to Government Valley Road. Follow this road 2.1 miles north to the campground. Hikers could also use the Reuter Springs Trailhead across from Reuter Campground to access the trail system.

Loop A

0.0	Sundance trailhead at Sundance Campground.
1.2	Tent Canyon Trail. Follow this north and west.
5.3	Ogden Creek Trail. Follow this west.
8.9	Link with Upper Ogden Trail. Proceed south.
10.2	Link with Sand Pit Trail. Proceed east.
11.2	Reconnect with Tent Canyon Ridge Trail.
13.0	Reconnect with Sundance Trail.

Loop B

0.0	Sundance trailhead at Sundance Campground.
1.2	Tent Canyon Trail. Proceed north.
2.2	Tent Canyon Ridge Trail. Follow this west.
5.5	Sand Pit Trail. Follow south, then southeast.
8.0	Reconnect with Sundance Trail.
9.2	Sundance trailhead.

The hikes: Loop A departs from Sundance Campground and proceeds westerly along the Sundance Trail until it connects 1.2 miles later with the Tent Canyon Trail. Follow Tent Canyon for 4.1 miles until intersecting with the Ogden Creek Trail. Take this trail west for 3.6 miles until linking with the Upper Ogden Trail. Proceed south on Upper Ogden Trail for 1.3 miles to where the trail meets the Sand Pit Trail, at which point hikers should head east. About 1 mile later, hikers will connect with the Tent Canyon Ridge Trail, and should follow this 2 miles to the Sundance Trail, which returns to the campground.

A shorter route, **Loop B** also begins on the Sundance Trail and follows it for 1.2 miles. To make this loop, proceed north on the Tent Canyon Trail for 1 mile to a junction with the Tent Canyon Ridge Trail, from the west. Follow the latter for 3.3 miles to the intersection with the Sand Pit Trail. Proceed south, then southeast, on the Sand Pit Trail. After 2.5 miles you'll reach the Sundance Trail, which you can take back to the campground for a total loop hike of 9.2 miles.

4   *REUTER SPRINGS TRAIL*

General description: A hike through a pine
forest on a ridge above
Reuter Canyon.

See Map on Page 23

Length: 2.9 miles (4.6 km) one way.
Difficulty: Moderately easy.
Trail maintenance: Yearly.
Traffic: Light.
Maps: USDA Forest Service brochure from Sundance
Forest Service office.

Finding the trailhead: From the Forest Service office on U.S. Highway 14 (Cleveland Street) near the east end of Sundance, proceed 2.9 miles (4.6 km) west on US 14 to Forest Road 838 north. Follow the road 2.6 miles (4.1 km) to Reuter Campground. The trail is accessed from FR 838, across the road from the campground entrance.

    0.0   Trailhead.
    2.9   End of Reuter Springs Trail.

The hike: The Reuter Springs Trail is suitable for hikers, horseback riders, and mountain bikers. Portions of this fairly new trail were developed in 1995.

The trail proceeds north from the trailhead and follows the ridge above Reuter Canyon. After 0.75 mile, openings in the ponderosa woods grant beautiful southern vistas of surrounding mountains and ranchlands. Signs of deer and elk are plentiful. The trail continues, winding around the canyon with moderate ascents.

At the northern terminus, hikers have several options. It is possible to link up with several of the Sundance trails, which head north and east, or return to Reuter Campground. From there you can cross FR 838, walk south on the road for 0.5 mile, and take the Carson Draw ski trail back to the campground again, paralleling the road. Another option is to simply retrace your route.

BEAR BUTTE STATE PARK

OVERVIEW

We did not think of the great open plains, the beautiful rolling hills, and the winding streams with tangled growth, as wild. Earth was bountiful and we were surrounded with the blessings of the great Mystery.

—Luther Standing Bear
Lakota Nation

Bear Butte is not a butte at all, but a mountain of igneous rock, formed in much the same way many other area mountains were sculpted. Bear Butte was born more than two million years ago when molten lava pushed into the surrounding land. Over the eons, the softer sedimentary rock engulfing the lava washed away, exposing the igneous core and creating a formation known as a laccolith. Bear Butte shares this manner of development with Crow Peak, among other local landmarks.

Although Bear Butte is not part of the Black Hills proper, its inclusion in this guidebook is justified for several reasons. Historically, it stood as a land-

To Native Americans, Bear Butte remains a spiritual area, one in which trails approach sweat lodges and other prayer areas. Respect cautionary signs that ask for silence and that unauthorized hikers maintain their distance.

mark, pointing the way for many early day "hikers" trudging across the prairie in search of gold, furs, or homesteads in the Black Hills. Because of its prominence and beauty, the butte has served as a beacon. It still does. Rising 1,200 feet above the plains, it is located just outside the northeast corner of the Black Hills, approximately 6 miles northeast of Sturgis, South Dakota, and is part of Bear Butte State Park. More recently, Bear Butte was designated as the northern terminus for the Centennial Trail, which courses more than 100 miles through the Black Hills.

In 1965 the mountain was designated a registered National Landmark because of its exceptional value in illustrating a unique segment of the natural history of the United States. In 1973 Bear Butte was placed on the National Register of Historic Places, because of its service as a beacon and its spiritual significance to Native Americans. Bear Butte was a magnet for Native Americans. The Cheyenne called the mountain Noavosse, meaning "Good Mountain," while the Lakota called it Mato Paha, or "Bear Mountain." Visiting the butte, Cheyenne medicine man Sweet Medicine received the four sacred Cheyenne arrows and a code of ethics for his people.

Native Americans who came here long ago generally climbed the mountain for spiritual reasons. Today they do much the same. We who follow in their footsteps should do so with a degree of humility, for Bear Butte is to many a cathedral, designated as such with much the same sense of reverence that leaders from the Christian community have declared certain temples to be sacred. We discuss the trail here, overcoming our concerns that publicity will contribute to a desecration of this Native American shrine. We believe and hope that as we hikers observe a sense of decorum, our presence will become acceptable.

Spiritual leaders ask that, as you hike the trails at Bear Butte, you comport yourself with reserve and some degree of somberness. Doing so, you may also feel the spirituality of the mountain. Observe off-limits signs and do not intrude on those who may be praying and meditating. Take only scenic photos and none of ceremonial objects or the Native Americans themselves.

Native Americans have tied prayer flags and bundles in trees over the many years of use, and these now number in the thousands. If viewed in the spirit of a naturalist—as one communing with nature—the flags' presence adds to the beauty of the hike and to an appreciation of its antiquity. Do not disturb them.

BEAR BUTTE

Talus Slope   Platform

Summit Trail

Chimney Rock

Platform

Summit
4,426 ft.

Centennial Trail

Ceremonial Trail

N

Trail
Contact
Station

Parking Lot

Visitor
Center

To
Newell

79

34

34

To
Rapid
City

Bear Butte Lake

Centennial Trail

Sturgis

79

90

To
Belle Fourche

34

90

14

To
Whitewood & Spearfish

5   BEAR BUTTE

General description:	A 2-hour hike from the base to the peak of a sacred mountain. The trail winds through a pine forest; many tree branches are draped with prayer flags and ceremonial objects.
Length:	3.75 miles (6.03 km) loop.
Difficulty:	Moderately strenuous to strenuous, due to the sharp ascent over a relatively short distance.
Trail maintenance:	Excellent.
Traffic:	Light to moderate.
Elevation gain:	1,026 feet.
Highest elevation:	4,426 feet.
Maps:	USDA Forest Service Centennial Trail User Guide. Bear Butte State Park management has provided a sketch map of the trails on an information sign at the trailhead.

Bear Butte

Finding the trailhead: From Sturgis (17 miles east of Spearfish on Interstate 90, or 27 miles west of Rapid City), take South Dakota Highway 34 east for 4 miles to South Dakota Highway 79. Go north on SD 79 for 4 miles to the sign on the right for Bear Butte State Park, where there is camping along the shores of Bear Butte Lake (across SD 79 from the park entrance).

One trailhead is at a parking lot 1 mile above the park visitor center. Another trailhead is located directly across Highway 79 from the turn-in for the state park. This is the Centennial Trail, and hikers could add 1.5 miles to their hike by departing from here.

    0.0   Trailhead.
    0.5   First overlook platform.
    1.3   Second overlook platform.
    1.6   Summit.

The hike: Bear Butte State Park's visitor center explains more about the area's natural history and its significance to Native Americans. Outside the visitor center is a bust of Frank Fools Crow (1809-1989), the ceremonial chief of the Teton Lakota Sioux and a nephew of Black Elk. The park's relatively short, steep system of three trails provides an excursion imbued with beauty and spirituality. Simultaneously the trail provides access to the top of Bear Butte, which offers unspoiled panoramic views.

Though you have options, you might begin the hike on the Ceremonial Trail, which is well marked at the trailhead. The dirt path is wide and ascends through stands of pine, crossing talus slopes and offering numerous switchbacks. As you begin the trek, almost immediately on your right you will see an old ring of stones once used for weighting the sides of a traditional teepee. The hill on the left is called Teaching Hill. This is where the Sioux leader Crazy Horse spoke to tribes gathered for a huge council in 1857. The meeting unified the Sioux in their resolve to not sell the Black Hills to the U.S. government. Here, jagged limestone formations rise in front of the trail.

Follow the Ceremonial Trail for 0.5 mile to where the first of three overlook platforms is located. Benches are provided on the overlook sites for resting and meditation. At this point hikers can continue up to the peak on the Summit Trail (which is also the Centennial Trail; see Hike 54), or descend on the Centennial Trail to the parking lot, making a short loop hike of under 1 mile. However, it is well worth the effort to continue to the peak.

The Summit Trail continues winding through pines and around the cliffs, with numerous switchbacks. Where washouts might occur, park managers have placed log steps. The second lookout is reached after another 0.8 mile and hikers find themselves standing above an enormous talus slope. Hikers reach the summit 0.45 mile later and are rewarded with commanding 360-degree views of bison, ponds, farms, and cattle; of the Black Hills looming to the southwest; and of the Badlands to the east.

From the peak, retrace the hike along the Summit Trail and descend to the first viewing platform. From there, choose your route, selecting either the Centennial Trail (0.25 mile) or the Ceremonial Trail (0.5 mile) to return to the parking lot.

On the day of our hike, a mist shrouded the land, but did not obscure the distant features. Rather, it combined with the golden leaves and served to heighten the mystery and spirituality of the area. I met Ralph Pretty Fox at Bear Butte on another day, in September, when snow was falling. He must have noticed the dreamcatcher hanging on the mirror in my van, since he waved at me as I stepped from the vehicle. His brown face was lined, and his head was crowded with a full crop of black hair tinged with silver. He said he was traveling home to Idaho but had stopped at Bear Butte for spiritual rejuvenation. We spoke quietly for a few moments, and then he said he would be returning in the evening for a sweat in one of the lodges below us and that I was welcome to join him.

I thanked Pretty Fox, but told him I could not make a commitment. "The weather," I said, motioning to the falling snow, covering the leaves of green and gold.

He asked me to walk with him for a moment down a trail, where he picked some sage. He rolled the fragrant leaves between his palms. Then he moved his hands in the four directions and asked me to meditate with him. Finally, Pretty Fox placed the sage in my left palm and crossed my right palm over the left, joining my hands. "Burn this for good luck as you travel," he said.

I thanked him, but said little. I wished I had something to give him in return.

DEVILS TOWER NATIONAL MONUMENT

OVERVIEW

Devils Tower rises abruptly in northeast Wyoming. The national monument—our nation's first—looms high above the land, and in so doing makes us wonder endlessly about its origin. Hikers who tread these trails walk through millions of years of the earth's past as well as more recent human history.

Because of the tower's shape and numerous striations, Native Americans sought spiritual interpretations of this most prominent of Wyoming edifices. In his book *The Way to Rainy Mountain*, N. Scott Momaday, a Pulitzer prize-winning novelist, recalled a story told by his grandmother. Her words carried a legend of a boy who had been turned into a bear:

Eight children were there at play, seven sisters and their brother. Suddenly the boy was struck dumb; he trembled and began to run upon his hand and feet. His fingers became claws, and his body was covered with fur....The sisters were terrified; they ran, and the bear after them. They came to the stump of a great tree, and the tree spoke to them. It bade them climb upon it, and as they did so it began to rise into the air. The bear came to kill them, but they were just beyond its reach. It reared against the tree and scored the bark all around with its claws. The seven sisters were borne into the sky, and they became the stars of the Big Dipper.

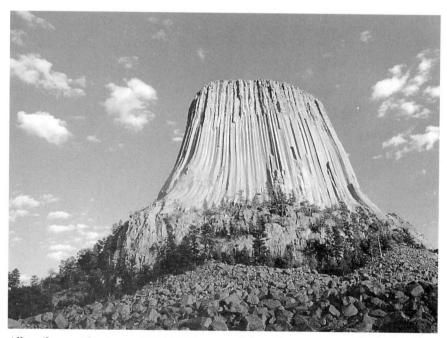

All trails provide views of Devils Tower, some close up.

DEVIL'S TOWER NATIONAL MONUMENT

Because of this legend, so eloquently presented by Momaday, Native Americans once referred to Devils Tower as Mateo Teepee, or "Bear's Lodge."

As appealing as the legend is, geologic science offers a somewhat different version of the tower's origin. Geologists say that forces deep within the earth pushed molten rock up until it was embraced by surrounding landforms. As the molten mass cooled, it condensed and cracked along joints, creating four-, five-, and six-sided rock columns—the striations you can see on the tower today. (These columns do occasionally fall, as evidenced by the piles of rocks that rim the tower's base. However, tests conducted to age lichens growing on the fallen rocks suggest the last column to fall did so about ten thousand years ago.).

Next came the forces of erosion. Since the molten intrusion was harder than the rock and soil of the surrounding landscape, water and wind acted on the softer soil and wore it away. With time—about 60 million years—soil and rocks that had once engulfed the molten columns melted away, leaving only the massive, weather-resistant projection that we see now. In human terms, the immense time frame for such sculpting of Devils Tower suggests inexorable forces. These processes are still in action, though the Black Hills are in no danger of losing the immense tower that dominates Wyoming's northeastern landscape anytime soon.

Devils Tower rises 867 feet from its base, 1,267 feet above the Belle Fourche River, and 5,117 feet above sea level. Because of its imposing nature and its stable rock, more than six thousand climbers attempt to scale its heights each year, and at least two hundred routes so far have been established. The tower was first climbed on July 4, 1893, with the aid of a ladder.

The monolith has long been revered by Native Americans, and in recent years some shift in management has occurred. Today the monument is managed for its spiritual significance as well. Signs near the tower remind visitors not to disturb prayer flags and bundles.

Although many come here to scale Devils Tower, the landscape surrounding the tower should not go unnoticed. Almost 8 miles of trails exist in the national monument. With the exception of one trail, all circle Devils Tower, providing views from every point of the compass. The trails here also provide exquisite, sweeping views of the nearby Belle Fourche River.

Simultaneously, they provide an opportunity for detailed studies of black-tailed prairie dogs and other Great Plains residents. Along the monument's trail, prairie dogs are easily approached; listen to their various calls as you hike the trail. More than seven distinctive chirps have been identified. If a coyote approaches or a hawk is spotted circling overhead, out goes an alarm signal, distinguished by two high-pitched notes. Likewise prairie dogs emit calls signifying contentment. While hiking in the prairie dog colonies, be aware that prairie rattlesnakes and black widow spiders make their homes in abandoned holes and tunnels. You may find nature's various nuances to be just as interesting as watching the many tower climbers.

The National Park Service lists five trails at the Monument, totaling nearly 8 miles (12.8 km). All are well marked and maintained. All trails at Devils Tower are relatively short, and though several climb rather steeply, none do

TOWER TRAIL
RED BEDS TRAIL
SOUTH SIDE AND VALLEY VIEW TRAILS
JOYNER RIDGE TRAIL

so for long. As a result, hikers need not possess Herculean strength or endurance. Anyone in reasonably good shape can hike here, even though trails such as the Red Beds Trail make quick elevation gains, climbing in places as much as 400 feet in short distances. As a result, we believe certain Devils Tower trails should be ranked moderately strenuous.

6   TOWER TRAIL

General description:	A popular circuit trail around the base of Devils Tower.
Length:	1.25 miles (2 km) round-trip.
Difficulty:	Easy.
Trail maintenance:	Good.
Traffic:	Heavy.
Maps:	Free trail brochure with map, available at entrance gate and visitor center.

Finding the trailhead: Devils Tower is 27 miles (43.4 km) northwest of Sundance, Wyoming, along U.S. Highway 14 and South Dakota Highway 24, and 107 miles (172 km) west and north of Rapid City, South Dakota. Take Interstate 90 west from Rapid City for 80 miles to US 14, then head north for 21 miles to SD 24, and go north for 6 miles. The trail begins at the visitor center, which is 3 miles (5 km) from the entrance gate.

The hike: The Tower Trail is perhaps the area's most popular because it most closely rings the base of Devils Tower and provides hikers with a good view of climbers as they scale the vertical columns. Along the way, the park provides benches and interpretive signs. About midway, the park provides a mounted set of viewing binoculars.

The path wanders through boulder fields and passes through stands of ponderosa pine, typical of other Black Hills vegetation. The trail also approaches columns that have sloughed off over the millennia and which, in turn, have been modified by the weather. Geologically, this trail excites those with a scientific bent and stirs the imagination in all who hike here.

The entire trail is paved, though somewhat bumpy. On the southeast side, a viewing tube focuses on the remains of the old ladder used in 1893 for the first tower climb. Doves wing along the columns, and vultures often mass near the top.

7   RED BEDS TRAIL

General description:	A longer hike around the tower base, past red sandstone formations and a prairie dog town.
Length:	2.8 miles (4.5 km) round-trip.
Difficulty:	Easy to moderately strenuous.
Trail maintenance:	Good.
Traffic:	Moderate.
Maps:	Free trail brochure with map, available at entrance gate and visitor center.

Finding the trailhead: The trail can be accessed from the visitor center (see Hike 6) or from one of the park's other trails that depart from the campground located about 0.5 mile from the entrance station.

- 0.0   Start.
- 0.7   Prairie dog town.
- 1.2   Belle Fourche River.
- 2.8   Trail's end.

The hike: The Red Beds Trail also rings Devils Tower, but from a greater distance. Beginning at the visitor center and proceeding south (counterclockwise), the trail descends slightly. Rock formations soon obscure Devils Tower. In 0.7 mile, the trail skirts a prairie dog community then lives up to its name as it passes through formations of red rocks (the red beds).

In another 0.5 mile the trail parallels the Belle Fourche River, then ascends several hundred feet where it once again approaches Devils Tower.

8   SOUTH SIDE AND VALLEY VIEW TRAILS

General description:	Two short, scenic trails near the tower's base.
Length:	Each trail is 0.6 mile (0.9 km) one way.
Difficulty:	Easy.
Trail maintenance:	Good.
Traffic:	Moderate.
Maps:	Free trail brochure with map, available at entrance gate and visitor center.

> *See Map on Page 35*

Finding the trailhead: Both trails begin at the Devils Tower amphitheater, which is near the campground about 0.5 mile from the monument's entrance.

The hike: Both the South Side and Valley View trails are one-way routes that must be retraced to the campground if hikers insist on maintaining the integrity of each trail's name. Both trails also wander through a black-tailed prairie dog town. The Valley View trail lives up to its name by providing elevated views of the nearby river and valley.

Those not insistent on hiking each trail by name might consider departing the Valley View Trail and linking with the Red Beds Trail, which circles Devils Tower then returns to the campground by following the South Side Trail for a total hike of 3 miles.

See Map on Page 35

General description:	A loop hike that provides more distant perspectives of Devils Tower and stunning views of the monument's three major ecosystems.
Length:	1.5-mile (2.4-km) loop.
Difficulty:	Easy to moderately strenuous.
Trail maintenance:	Good.
Traffic:	Light.
Maps:	Free trail brochure with map, available at entrance gate and visitor center.

Finding the trailhead: Access this trail by following the park's road from the entrance station for 2 miles until it intersects with West Road, on the left. Take West Rd. 0.5 mile to the trailhead.

The hike: The loop known as Joyner Ridge Trail is most easily hiked in a clockwise direction. Hikers pass through the three major Devils Tower ecosystems on this route, including prairie, riparian, and ponderosa pine habitats. Deer abound throughout. The trail is well marked with signs along the way, interpreting the natural communities and enhancing nature's abundant manifestations. Keep alert for prairie rattlesnakes.

SPEARFISH AREA

The Spearfish Canyon area is so unique that a National Scenic Byway winds 18 miles between the canyon walls and among tree-covered slopes, providing a tour of unparalleled beauty. Hikers would be wise to drive this road, since it gives an excellent overview of this section of the Black Hills, which is managed as part of Black Hills National Forest.

Spearfish Canyon formations began to take shape thirty to sixty million years ago. Geologically, three types of rocks dominate the canyon's walls and can be clearly viewed in several places. The top (and thickest and oldest) layer is of the Paha Sapa limestone and is usually gray. The middle layer is Englewood limestone and consists of reddish hues. The bottom is brown, layered, and referred to as Deadwood shale. Vertically formed dark gray rocks called igneous intrusions may also be seen in some areas. Bridal Veil Falls drop from a formation that is a prime example of this condition.

Botanically, four distinctly different vegetative regions thrive in the canyon, which in itself is unusual. The area is a meeting place for plants, trees, and bushes from the Great Plains, the Rocky Mountains, and the Eastern deciduous and Northern forests. No clear explanation exists for such diversity, though it probably derives from ancient climactic changes.

Another novelty, according to one brochure, is that Spearfish Creek is the only known river in the region that freezes from the bottom up. Just how the creek actually received its name is not known, but it is said that Native Americans liked to spear the native long-nosed dace and mountain suckers in the unclouded waters. Today, the clear waters are filled with rainbow, brown, and brook trout, which were introduced in 1899.

Several trails exist side-by-side in Spearfish Canyon, including the Little Spearfish Trail, the Rimrock Trail Upper Loop, and the Rimrock Trail Lower Loop. These are high-country hikes, passing through stands of aspen, birch, pine, and spruce. Each provides both beauty and tranquillity. The winter scenes of the movie *Dances With Wolves* were filmed in this canyon, and with a little imagination the tepees pitched in the snow and the drama portrayed of those long-ago times can be conjured easily. A small sign indicates the filming area, but there is fortunately no other hype about what occurred here.

Two campgrounds, Rod and Gun Campground and Timon Campground, are free after Labor Day; water is usually turned off at that time. Trail users who are not camping should avoid parking in the campgrounds during the fee season (Memorial Day through Labor Day).

SPEARFISH AREA

General description:	A full-day hike winding upwards through pine forests to fantastic panoramas at the summit, and back.
Length:	7 miles (11.2 km) round-trip.
Difficulty:	Moderately strenuous to strenuous.
Trail maintenance:	Excellent.
Traffic:	Moderate.
Elevation gain:	1,560 feet.
Highest elevation:	5,760 feet.
Maps:	Black Hills National Forest Map; USDA Crow Peak Trail Map No. 64 and Black Hills National Forest handout of Spearfish Trails, available free at area Forest Service offices and visitor centers.

Crow Peak Trail

CROW PEAK TRAIL LOCATOR

Finding the trailhead: The trailhead is 6.9 miles (11.1 km) west of Spearfish off Interstate 90 via Exit 10. Take Utah Street (one block east of the Forest Service office) west for 2.6 miles past a four-way stop sign. Take a left on Higgins Gulch Road (Forest Road 214, a good gravel road) and follow it for 3.9 miles to the trailhead and a large parking area, on the right.

0.0	Trailhead.
1.5	Spur Trail to Beaver Ridge.
3.5	Crow Peak.
7.0	Trailhead.

The hike: Crow Peak Trail is a popular hike. The trail winds up to the mountaintop, providing sweeping vistas at the summit. Crow Peak is so named because of a battle once fought here between the Crow and Sioux Indians. Appropriately, the mountain in Sioux tongue, Paha Karitukateyapi, translates to "the place where the Sioux killed the Crow."

CROW PEAK TRAIL

3.5 Miles from Trailhead to Crow Peak

Crow Peak is an igneous intrusion and was formed in the same manner as Bear Butte and several other peaks in the area. Eons ago, molten magma filled limestone and sedimentary layers, which then cooled to form the hard igneous rock. Erosion and washing away of sedimentary deposits continues to reform the hills in the area.

The trail begins in Higgins Gulch amidst ponderosa pine woods and much new growth of native bushes and bur oak. The 3.5 miles up the peak go moderately in some places, strenuously in others. The route heads west on the southern side of the hill and climbs ever upward. The trail is well-blazed on trees with one large rectangle directly below a smaller rectangle.

At about 1.5 miles you encounter a junction. Here you might want to take the 1-mile round-trip Beaver Ridge spur trail to the south. If not, continue in a northerly direction toward the summit.

As the trail nears the top, the forest thins and the path becomes more rocky. Simultaneously the trail offers the promise of spectacular views ahead—and at the peak lives up to its promise.

Our hike occurred on a mid-September day when several inches of early snow covered the peak. Where valleys retained pockets of cold, snow had lingered. At the summit, the contrast between the valley and the peak was dramatic. Below, fall had barely tinged the trees, but several thousand feet higher, fall and winter were already colliding. The view from the top is almost surreal.

Lookout, Spearfish, and Terry peaks as well as Bear Butte and other high points appear in the east. The plains of eastern Montana and the Bearlodge Mountains of Wyoming lie to the west, with Warren Peak sometimes visible. Spread below is the town of Spearfish, nestled in all this beauty.

Crow Peak Trail is designated for hikers and horsebackers only. The trail exhibits but little evidence of horse use and the typical erosion that often results from the tread of heavy animals is absent. Because the trail is steep, hikers might become dehydrated. Carry an ample supply of drinking water.

11   OLD BALDY TRAIL

General description:	A mountain loop hike with an optional spur trail to the summit of Old Baldy, offering sweeping views of the northern Black Hills.
Length:	6.1-mile (9.8-km) loop; 0.8-mile (1.3 km) spur.
Difficulty:	Easy to moderate.
Trail maintenance:	Excellent.
Traffic:	Moderate.
Elevation gain:	300 feet.
Highest elevation:	6,096 feet.
Maps:	Black Hills National Forest Map; Old Baldy Trail Map No. 66; USDA Black Hills National Forest handout, available free at area Forest Service offices and visitor centers.

Finding the trailhead: From Spearfish, take Forest Road 134 (Tinton Road) south for 13 miles (20.9 km) to the trailhead, on the right. Or take the Spearfish Canyon National Scenic Byway (U.S. Highway 14A) south from Spearfish for 12.8 miles to Savoy. At Savoy, take Forest Road 222 (a good gravel road) south for 6 miles. Turn right on FR 134 and follow it for 1.2 miles to the trailhead on the left.

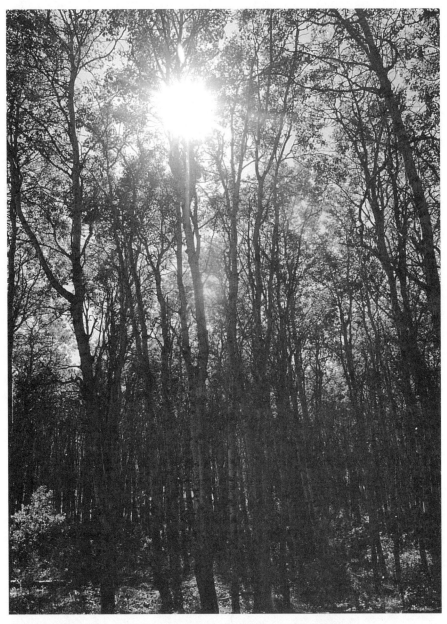

Sunlight filters through the trees along the trail to Old Baldy.

The trail also can be accessed (adding about 2 miles to the hike) by following the above directions to FR 222, then parking at the Little Spearfish Trailhead, adjacent to Timon Campground. From here, hikers should take the Rimrock Trail Upper Loop north for 1 mile to a marker for Old Baldy Trail, near a quarry on the left. Another mile of hiking brings you to the trailhead and route described below.

OLD BALDY TRAIL

0.0   Trailhead.
1.25 Lap Circle Ranch.
2.25 Old Baldy Trail Junction.
3.0   Old Baldy.
3.75 Old Baldy Trail Junction.
4.0   Old Baldy Lake.
5.9   Trailhead.

Old Baldy Trail

The hike: The Old Baldy Trail is a combination loop and spur trail that meanders through prime deer and elk habitat. Throughout the hike the trail is exceptionally well marked. Blazes are abundant and the grade is gentle. The trail could make for an ideal family outing, particularly for those interested in the possibility of observing wildlife. From Old Baldy Mountain, the vistas are satisfying, offering views to the east of Ragged Top and Terry Peak; to the west hikers can view Cement Ridge Lookout. Crow Peak looms in the north, a mountain with a geological background similar to that of Old Baldy.

The Old Baldy Trail, if followed along the western route, begins in a beautiful grove of aspens that includes much park-like terrain. The combination, with its understory of buckthorn (*Ceanothus*) provides ideal winter habitat for elk, whose tracks and droppings are often abundant. For backpackers, numerous campsites exist because the terrain is relatively flat.

About 0.75 mile from the trailhead, the path descends gently and progresses north, crossing a broad bench. The trail then proceeds northwesterly for 0.5 mile, paralleling the fence line of the Lap Circle Ranch. The trail swings southeast and ascends several hundred feet to a small bench where it then turns to the north.

The trail intersects with the Old Baldy Spur 0.75 mile later, then ascends 0.8 mile to the summit. The ascent is gentle and the climb can be completed quickly. Though Old Baldy Mountain is little more than a knob, the views are sweeping and encompass much of the Black Hills foothills as well as the peaks mentioned above. Botanically, the peak itself is classified as a dry-site environment, for the vegetation consists of ponderosa pine over an understory of mountain balm and some Oregon grape.

Retracing the 0.8-mile spur to the intersection, the return trip to the trailhead is but 2 miles. From the intersection, within 0.25 mile, the trail passes a small "lake" called Baldy Lake, created by a man-made dike. The resulting pond serves as a water hole for cattle, but judging from the abundant deer tracks it also serves wildlife. The country here consists of open park-like areas and again provides ideal habitat for ungulates.

Shortly after passing Baldy Lake, the trail veers south and ascends via a series of gentle switchbacks to a small knob almost as high as Old Baldy. About 1 mile later the east route concludes at the trailhead.

General description:	A three- to five-hour loop hike that rambles through ponderosa pine forest and ends near a great walk-in fishing area.
Length:	5.7-mile (9.2-km) loop.
Difficulty:	Moderate to easy.
Trail maintenance:	Good.
Traffic:	Moderate (people and deer).
Elevation gain:	800 feet.
Highest elevation:	6,280 feet.
Maps:	Black Hills National Forest Map; Little Spearfish Trail Map No. 80 and a free Black Hills National Forest handout, available at nearby Forest Service offices and visitor centers.

Finding the trailhead: Take U.S. Highway 14A (Spearfish Canyon National Scenic Byway) south from Spearfish for 12.8 miles (20.5 km) to Savoy, or take US 14A northwest from Cheyenne Crossing (the southern terminus of the scenic byway) for 5.7 miles to Savoy. Then follow Forest Road 222 south about 4 miles to the north side of Timon Campground, where the main trailheads for Hikes 12 and 13 are located. The trails can also be accessed from several points along FR 222 (signs are posted along the way). Rod and Gun Campground is 2 miles down FR 222, offering access to both loops of the Rimrock Trail (Hike 13).

     0.0   Trailhead.
     0.8   Road crossing.
     3.0   Highest elevation.
     5.7   Trailhead.

The hike: Beginning at Little Spearfish trailhead adjacent to Timon Campground, the trail proceeds east in the woods toward Ranger Draw, paralleling FR 222 for about 0.8 mile. Cross the road twice, and at the second crossing pick up the trail again about 10 yards to the right.

Soon the trail heads south, still in the woods, into a moderately steep ascent that soon becomes a gentle climb until you reach the highest elevation of 6,280 feet. The ponderosa pines here are quite tall and not crowded. The trail is well worn through this lush setting, which is perfect elk and deer habitat.

About 3 miles from the start, the trail levels and swings sharply west-northwest. At this point, hikers encounter a dirt road and wire fence. Stay to the north (right) of the fence and look for blazes on the trees. Often the blazes are difficult to see, since they are cut into the tree bark. The next mile of trail descends through more elk and deer habitat.

The final mile, which is flat, wanders through meadows along Little

LITTLE SPEARFISH TRAIL
RIMROCK TRAIL

To Old Baldy Trail

134.2

Ⓑ Lower Loop

Rod and Gun Campground

To Savoy

Ⓑ

Ⓑ

Upper Loop

Ⓑ

222.1

222.1

223

Ⓐ

Timon Campground

Ⓐ

N

Ⓐ

Ⓐ Little Spearfish Trail 5.7 Miles
Ⓑ Rimrock Trail
  Lower Loop   3.5 Miles
  Upper Loop   4.5 Miles

Spearfish Creek and the walk-in fishing area. Those who like to fish will want to pack in a pole (and South Dakota license), since the trout are often visible in the abundant pools.

13   RIMROCK TRAIL

General description:	Two loops or a combined circuit hike through large stands of ponderosa, aspen, and birch, with views of limestone cliffs.
Length:	It is possible to make two loops here: an Upper Loop of 4.5 miles (7.24 km) and a Lower Loop of 3.5 miles (5.6 km). Hikers can also eliminate the common middle section and hike the combined outer segments of both loops for a total of 6.5 miles (10.5 km).
Difficulty:	Upper Loop, moderately strenuous; Lower Loop, moderate.
Trail maintenance:	Good.
Traffic:	Moderate.
Elevation gain:	Upper Loop, 450 feet; Lower Loop, 720 feet.
Highest elevation:	6,040 feet.
Maps:	Black Hills National Forest Map; Rimrock Trail No. 79 Map; Black Hills National Forest handout, available free from Forest Service offices, trailhead boxes, and visitor centers.

Upper Loop

0.0	Trailhead.
0.75	Old Baldy Trail junction.
2.5	Ranger Station.
4.5	Trailhead.

Lower Loop

0.0	Trailhead.
0.8	Canyon rim.
3.5	Trailhead.

Rimrock Trail No. 79

The hike: To hike the **Upper Loop**, depart from the Little Spearfish Trailhead (adjacent to Timon Campground) and make an initial climb to the north for about 100 yards. The ascent is quite steep and strenuous at first, then levels off to a gradual climb as the trail angles through the woods.

After 0.75 mile, the junction for Old Baldy trailhead to the west is encountered near the site of an old rock quarry. You've reached the maximum elevation now of 6,040 feet, and here the Rimrock Trail levels out, heading north and east.

More trail junctions occur in another 0.75 mile. To complete the Upper Loop, head east, following the sign for the Rod and Gun Campground, reached in 1 mile. At this point, about 2 miles remain to the trailhead, all of it level hiking that parallels bubbling Little Spearfish Creek, as well as FR 222. Along the route you'll see part of an old ranger station foundation and an old stone root cellar. The trail crosses the road three times before concluding back at Timon Campground.

The **Lower Loop** is the shorter of the two loop trails. To take this route, begin your hike at the Rod and Gun Campground. The trail begins at the west end of the campground, passes through a cattle gate, then ascends immediately for about 0.8 mile to the rim of the canyon, in a westerly direction. It then levels out through ponderosa pine, quaking aspen, and stands of birch for about 0.5 mile. Deer tracks abound, and flickers dart among the tree branches. The variation and abundance of plant life in this area is amazing and includes juniper, sage, varied wildflowers, buck brush, and kinnikinnick, a favorite grouse dish. The remainder of the trail provides a gradual descent into the depths of Little Spearfish Canyon, where the rock walls and formations stand in mute testimony to the forces of nature. A brief hike through tall grasses returns hikers to the trailhead.

The combined loops of the Rimrock Trail are designed for hikers, horsebackers, and mountain bikers. Horse use appears light, with no evidence of trail erosion.

14   BIG HILL TRAILS

General description:	A connecting series of trails at the summit of Big Hill, taking hikers through beautiful stands of quaking aspen, paper birch, and ponderosa pine and past sporadic views of the surrounding area.
Length:	Five loops of various lengths, covering a total of 16.5 miles (26.5 km).
Difficulty:	Easy to moderate.
Trail maintenance:	Good.
Traffic:	Light; heavier in winter for cross-country skiing.
Elevation gain:	400 feet.
Highest elevation:	5,400 feet.
Maps:	Black Hills National Forest Map; Big Hill Trail Map No. 72; a free Black Hills National Forest handout is available at area Forest Service offices, the trailhead box, or nearby visitor centers.

Big Hill Trails

Finding the trailhead: From Spearfish, take Jackson Boulevard, which crosses Main Street in the center of town, southwest to the top of the hill. Follow signs to the left for Tinton Road (Forest Road 134), which is a good gravel road. Follow FR 134 for 7.8 miles to the top of Big Hill and the small parking lot on the right, which has a sign for Big Hill Trails. The trailheads are directly across the road.

BIG HILL TRAILS

Loop A.1	0.5 Mile
Loop A	2.1 Miles
Loop B	2.4 Miles
Loop C	5.5 Miles
C.1	1.5 Miles (one-way)
Loop D	4.5 Miles

The hikes: Fall is a perfect time to hike the many trails of this area as gold aspens and birches shimmer against the dark green ponderosa pines. Early in the morning, families of deer still browse and coyotes howl across the ridgetops. This is prime elk habitat, too.

This is rolling country, with the trails following the gentle slopes. All trails wander through the mixed stands of trees in the woods. Atop Big Hill solitude abounds and offers hikers a chance to enjoy the peace and a variety of views. According the Forest Service handout, Big Hill was so named long ago by miners heading south from Spearfish to the gold fields. With all the wagons and teams it was a real grind to make it over the big hill.

We sampled the area's trails by combining Loops A and B into one hike of about 3 miles. To access the loops, walk southeast a brief 0.25 mile where Loop A begins; taking the left fork brings you to Loop C, which runs to the rim of Spearfish Canyon, 1,000 feet deep. The right fork takes hikers to Loops B or C. Loop D is reached from the southern part of Loop C. Loop A is the shortest route at 2.1 miles (3.4 km.), and Loop C is the longest at 5.5 miles (8.8 km).

Big Hill Trails are designed for hikers, bikers, horsebackers, and cross-country skiers, and the area is designated "multiple use." The trails and loops are well marked with signposts and tree blazes.

15   EAGLE CLIFF TRAILS

General description:	An extensive series of twenty loop and one-way trails, originally designed for cross-country skiers but also used by hikers, mountain bikers, and horseback riders.
Length:	Various trails, ranging from 0.2 mile to 3.4 miles, in many combinations.
Difficulty:	Easy to moderately strenuous.
Elevation gain:	Up to 760 feet.
Highest elevation:	6,500 feet.
Maps:	Black Hills National Forest Map; Eagle Cliff Trail Map No. 68; free Black Hills National Forest handout, available at area Forest Service offices and visitor centers.

Eagle Cliff Trails

Finding the trailheads: From Spearfish, take U.S. Highway 14A (a National Scenic Byway) south for 22 miles (35.4 km) to Cheyenne Crossing. Then take U.S. Highway 85 south for 7.4 miles (11.9 km) to the first trailhead, or 8.4 miles (13.5 km) to the second trailhead. Both trailheads are north of the highway.

The hikes: This rugged, high, somewhat remote series of loop trails offers short trips of an hour or the opportunity to hike for several days. Many loop combinations are possible, and ambitious hikers may want to try one long perimeter hike. Unique trail names, such as "What The Hell," "Wipe Out," and "Deep Snow," reflect the fact that this system was begun by local cross-country skiers.

EAGLE CLIFF TRAILS

ADDITIONAL HIKES

Hikers may enjoy several other short hikes in the Spearfish area. Among them are the following.

Mount Roosevelt

A trail up Mount Roosevelt goes 0.5 mile (0.8 km) one-way to the top. Hikers can rest at the overlooks of Mount Roosevelt as the trail winds through stands of aspen and large boulders, offering grand views along the way and at the summit. The trail is an easy one, with an elevation gain of 150 feet and a maximum elevation of 5,600 feet.

The Mount Roosevelt trail makes a fun, easy jaunt for the entire family. The elevation gain is minimal, the views are nice, and the trail is a good one. Historic Friendship Tower atop the mountain was built by Seth Bullock, a Deadwood rancher, as a tribute to his deep friendship with President Theodore Roosevelt.

Mount Roosevelt is located a short distance northwest of Deadwood, South Dakota. To find the trailhead, take U.S. Highway 85 south from Interstate 90, just east of Spearfish. US 85 is well marked from I-90. Just before reaching the town of Deadwood, take Forest Road 133 west from US 85. Go approximately 3 miles and park in the lot at the picnic area.

Roughlock Falls

The Savoy area is a popular one for several reasons. Here, two huge canyons, Spearfish and Little Spearfish, come together to offer spectacular views. The ancient rock formations are a geologist's delight. And Little Spearfish Canyon offers wonderful hiking trails and fishing spots.

The trail to Roughlock Falls is a flat, 1-mile (1.6-km) walk along Spearfish Creek to the picturesque waterfall, which is a favorite picnic spot. The trail is easy and barrier free, accessible to visitors in wheelchairs. The cascading falls are charming at all times of the year. The falls are so named because, before the current road existed, the old wagon and log-sled path was very steep. Drivers "rough-locked" the wheels of their vehicles with ropes or chains so the wagons would drag instead of jacking out of control.

Roughlock Falls are located about 0.5 mile from Savoy on Forest Road 222. To reach Savoy, take U.S. Highway 14A (Spearfish Canyon National Scenic Byway) south from Spearfish for 12.8 miles. Drive about 0.5 mile south of Savoy on FR 222 to a parking area on your left. From here, you can hike a wide, tree-lined path for 1 mile along Spearfish Creek to Roughlock Falls.

CUSTER STATE PARK

OVERVIEW

In 1919, through the mighty efforts of South Dakota Governor Peter Norbeck and others, land that once had been a state game preserve became Custer State Park. Today the park contains 73,000 acres (29,543 hectares), consisting of grasslands, ponderosa pine forests, bur oak, and white spruce. As a wildlife preserve, Custer has one of the world's largest bison herds and is home to elk, deer, bighorn sheep, and even mountain goats. Custer is also one of the largest state parks in our nation. Appropriately, the park serves as an excellent area for recreation, offering trout fishing in its many streams and man-made lakes.

The park offers abundant camping spots and trails in both grasslands and forests. Though the trail system is not extensive, it is varied. Trails in Custer State Park wind through prairies, mountains, and incredible rock formations. They offer abundant views of wildlife, lakes, and streams. They're varied enough to let you hear the insects, to see the abundant wildlife, and to allow winds to shape your thoughts.

When hiking in Custer State Park, always be aware of the possibility of bison encounters. Never approach these huge, shaggy monarchs. A cow with her calf in the spring represents a threat, as do animals of both sexes in the mating season in July and August.

For the adventurer in search of a vignette of primitive America, a South

At one time bison in North America exceeded 30 million animals. Today bison still thunder across the trails in Custer State Park.

CUSTER STATE PARK

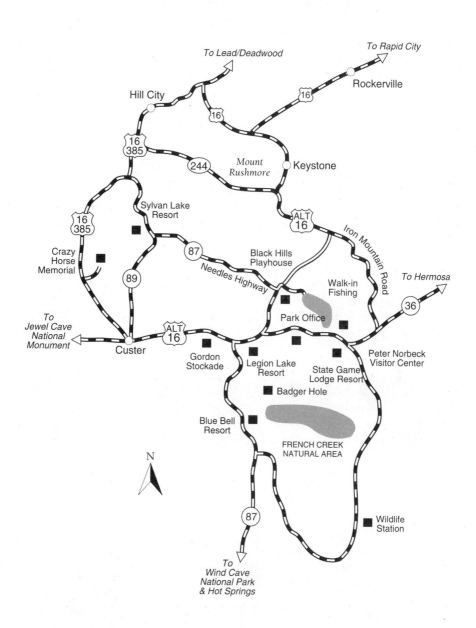

To Lead/Deadwood

To Rapid City

Hill City

Rockerville

16

16

16
385

244

Mount
Rushmore

Keystone

Sylvan Lake
Resort

16
385

ALT
16

Iron Mountain Road

Crazy
Horse
Memorial

87

Black Hills
Playhouse

Needles Highway

Walk-in
Fishing

To Hermosa

89

36

Park Office

To
Jewel Cave
National
Monument

ALT
16

Custer

Gordon
Stockade

Legion Lake
Resort

State Game
Lodge Resort

Peter Norbeck
Visitor Center

Badger Hole

Blue Bell
Resort

FRENCH CREEK
NATURAL AREA

N

87

Wildlife
Station

To
Wind Cave
National Park
& Hot Springs

Dakota that once was, the Black Hills offers few better examples. Though summer and fall are ideal times to hike here, we recommend fall as the best season. The days are cool, and the aspen, birch, and bur oak assume colors that reflect the presence of plant pigments other than just green chlorophyll.

Custer State Park is located in the southeast portion of the Black Hills, directly north of Wind Cave National Park and about a 45-minute drive south from Rapid City, South Dakota. From Interstate 90 at Rapid City, take South Dakota Highway 79 south for 17 miles. About 1 mile south of the town of Hermosa, follow South Dakota Highway 36 west for 9 miles to U.S. Highway 16A west, which will take you to the park's east entrance.

For an alternative scenic route, drive through the center of the Black Hills. To do so, proceed from Spearfish off I-90, taking U.S. Highway 85 south to U.S. Highway 385 south. Take US 16 east at the town of Custer into Custer State Park. If you are heading west take I-90 west to Sturgis, then take U.S. Highway 14 west toward Deadwood. Take US 385 south, following above suggestions from Spearfish. State highway maps show the numerous cutoffs to these routes, and signs pointing the way to Custer State Park can be found throughout the Black Hills.

Two visitor centers exist in the park. The Peter Norbeck Visitor Center is located on the park's main road (US 16A) about 3 miles west of the junction of South Dakota Highway 36 and US 16, and is open from May through October. The Wildlife Station Visitor Center is located on the eastern portion of the Wildlife Loop Road and is open from the end of May through Labor Day.

The bighorn sheep population in Custer numbers about 150 to 200.

CUSTER STATE PARK (DETAIL)

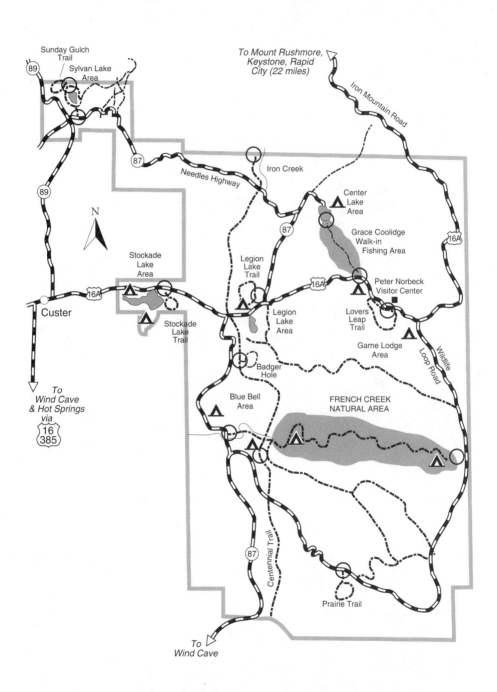

To become acquainted with the park and its multitudinous offerings, we found it helpful as well as rewarding to drive all three of the scenic roads provided to visitors. The vistas are incredible and, for those planning to hike, the drives furnish a good overview of trail locations (see overview map for road locations). The drives take longer than the mileages indicate because the roads are winding. The Needles Highway is 14 miles (22.5 km) long and curves its way around magnificent granite formations. The Iron Mountain Road is 16 miles (25.7 km) in length, with pigtail bridges and tunnels carved from the granite rock. This road leads from the park to Mount Rushmore. The 18-mile (28.9-km) Wildlife Loop Road shows another side of the park—its rolling prairie grasslands and their magnificent display of wildlife.

NOTE: Because trail elevations in Custer State Park vary less than 500 feet, we have not included trail profiles with the descriptions below.

16 FRENCH CREEK

General description:	An overbight backpack into a pristine natural area along a gorge of unique rock formations, with numerous creek fordings.
Length:	12 miles (19.3 km) one-way.
Difficulty:	Moderate.
Trail maintenance:	Only marked for 1 mile in from each terminus. Hikers must make their own way or follow the trails left by others.
Traffic:	Light to moderate.
Maps:	Trails Illustrated Topo Map No. 238; free Custer State Park Trail Guide, available at park visitor centers and entrances.

See Map on Page 63

Finding the trailhead: To reach the east trailhead, head east from Peter Norbeck Visitor Center on U.S. Highway 16A. Go 0.8 mile to the Wildlife Loop Road, on the right. Turn and follow this road south for 4 miles to the trailhead sign on the right.

To reach the west trailhead, continue south on Wildlife Loop Rd. to Blue Bell Lodge, a total of 20 miles. From here, take Custer State Park Road 4 (gravel) east for 3 miles to the trailhead.

0.0	Eastern terminus.
0.5	Stream disappears.
2.0	Primitive campground.
5.0	Sheer rock walls.
10.5	West end primitive campground.
12.0	Western terminus.

The hike: French Creek originates northwest of the town of Custer. It feeds Stockade Lake and continues its eastward flow, passing through Custer State Park. The creek cuts into the land, doing so in a dramatic manner through what Custer State Park has designated the French Creek Natural Area. Over its next 12 miles, the creek exposes some of the Black Hill's most spectacular granitic and sedimentary layers in the form of narrow defiles and cozy, colorful canyons. Surrounding walls rise boldly and radiate colors of red, orange, and yellow.

Near here, at the present site of the Gordon Stockade, a member of George Armstrong Custer's 1874 expedition to the Black Hills discovered gold, a presence that was to alter treaties and revise forever the interaction of native peoples and settlers here.

For the angler/hiker the French Creek area offers some of the state's best fishing. Brown and rainbow trout in the canyon's deep holes and numerous riffles respond well to dry flies and spinners. For the nature hiker, the canyons offer abundant wildlife sightings in the form of turkeys, deer, elk, and bands of bighorn sheep. In fall, bull elk lift their heads and bugle, and the canyon's walls ring to the sonorous cry of wandering males attempting to proclaim their territories and establish harems.

Here, too, is a geological phenomenon. Near the eastern end of the natural area, waters in French Creek disappear over a several hundred-yard span of stream only to reemerge several miles later with added vigor. Geologists call this phenomenon sinkhole topography, saying that in the distant millennia subsurface pockets were formed where soft sedimentary rock was engulfed by harder sedimentary rock. Eventually the soft rock eroded. The void was filled, in this case, by French Creek, particularly noticeable in the

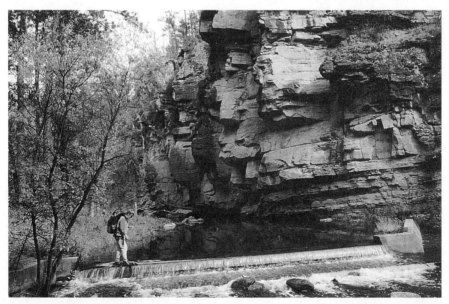

Stream crossing in the French Creek Natural Area.

drier season. But about 1 mile in from the eastern trailhead, the creek ceases in a very dramatic fashion: Now you see it, now you don't.

French Creek Natural Area offers two primitive camping sites. The easternmost site is just 1.5 miles from the trailhead at a place where the canyon narrows just beyond an abrupt turn of the creek. From the trailhead to this point, the path is a well-traveled one, but from here on hikers must sometimes create their own trails or follow those left by others. In one section of the French Creek hike, about 5 miles in from the eastern trailhead, hikers are challenged by sheer rock walls in a place called the Narrows. Since there is no place to walk, a swim or a very steep ascent around it is in order.

Paths generally parallel the creek until they approach the trail's western terminus some 10 miles later. Here, in the shadow of the Blue Bell area, about 1.5 miles from the western end, the park offers another primitive camping area. Hikers in French Creek are cautioned to maintain a watchful eye for bison and rattlesnakes, and to be aware of the abundance of poison ivy.

17 GRACE COOLIDGE WALK-IN FISHING AREA

General description:	A beautiful, fairly flat walk terminating at Center Lake, paralleling (with many crossings) Grace Coolidge Creek.
Length:	2.8 miles (4.5 km) one-way.
Difficulty:	Easy.
Trail maintenance:	Good.
Traffic:	Moderate.
Elevation gain:	Slight, less than 300 feet.
Maps:	Trails Illustrated Topo Map No. 238; free Custer State Park Trail Guide, available at visitor centers and entrance stations.

Trailhead location: To find the southern trailhead, take U.S. Highway 16A west from the Peter Norbeck Visitor Center for 1.5 miles. The trailhead is on the right, across the road from the Grace Coolidge Campground.

To access the northern trailhead, take US 16A west from visitor center to South Dakota Highway 87 north. Go 8 miles to the turnoff for Center Lake and the Black Hills Playhouse, then go in 1 mile to Center Lake. The trailhead is located by the shower house above the lake.

0.0   Southern trailhead.
2.8   Northern trailhead at Center Lake.

The hike: The Grace Coolidge Walk-in Fishing Area trail is actually an old, overgrown logging road. It is an easy and refreshing hike, and the numerous crossings over the narrow, sometimes deep, creek add to the fun.

FRENCH CREEK • GRACE COOLIDGE WALK-IN FISHING AREA • LOVERS' LEAP TRAIL • LEGION LAKE TRAIL • PRAIRIE TRAIL • BADGER CLARK HISTORIC TRAIL

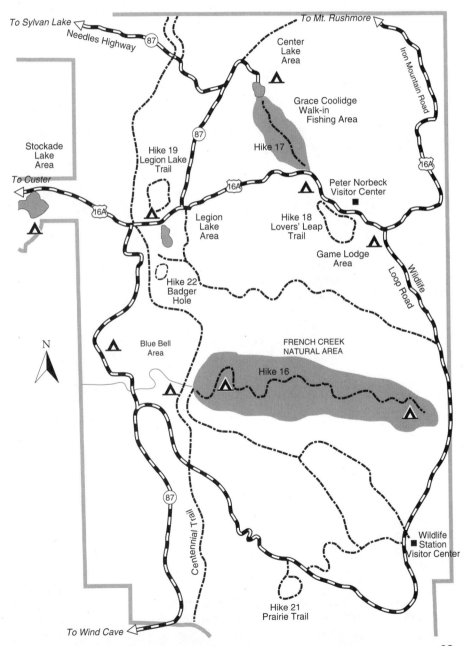

Seven low-head dams exist along the way, some with deep dark pools lying beneath granite rock formations. Walking and fishing along this trail is a fun outing for the entire family.

In summer, the trail is alive with the vibrant colors of wildflowers; in fall, the bur oak and birch tree leaves add a startling gold that contrasts with the green-black of the ponderosa pine. As in many low, wet areas, poison ivy is abundant along the trail and by the creek.

Photo opportunities abound here, as do chances for excellent fishing. The pools are stocked with brown and rainbow trout, so hiking anglers should be sure to pack in fishing gear along with their South Dakota license.

In 1927 President Calvin Coolidge and his family maintained a summer White House nearby; as a result, many features in the area bear the Coolidge name.

18   LOVERS' LEAP TRAIL

General description:	A 2- to 3-hour loop trail passing through pine and oak forest, offering great views at the summit.
Length:	4-mile (6.4-km) loop.
Difficulty:	Moderately strenuous for the first 30 minutes, then moderate to easy.
Trail maintenance:	Good.
Traffic:	Heavy.
Elevation gain:	480 feet.
Highest elevation:	4,780 feet.
Maps:	Trails Illustrated Topo Map No. 238; Custer State Park Trail Guide booklet, available at the park office, visitor centers, and entrances.

Finding the trailhead: The trail begins behind the schoolhouse across from the Peter Norbeck Visitor Center on U.S. Highway 16A, which is 3 miles east of the park entrance station off South Dakota Highway 36.

0.0	Trailhead.
2.0	Lovers' Leap Overlook.
2.5	Series of stream crossings begin.
4.0	Return to trailhead.

The hike: With lots of potential for a fun family outing, this hike combines gentle ups and downs after an initial steep ascent to a ridge; numerous stream crossings exist, though none are too difficult. Hikers should remain alert for poison ivy, which is abundant near the streams.

According to legend, Lovers' Leap derives its name from a Native American couple who elected to end their lives by plummeting from the lofty outcropping of rocks on a 200-foot ridge. Just why the couple leaped to their deaths is not remembered. Today, a lone ponderosa pine stands among the conglomerate rocks overlooking the sheer drop of several hundred feet. Not surprisingly, the ridge commands spectacular views of the Black Hills.

The overlook is reached by following the broad trail from the school-house where it immediately begins a 30- to 45-minute, relatively steep climb through bur oak and ponderosa pine forest. Prairie grasses mat the hillsides as you climb to the top. As you approach the summit, interesting rock formations and lichen-covered boulders are scattered on the hill to your right. The trail begins to level out as you near the site of Lovers' Leap.

At the trail's highest point, a sign greets you and provides the following message: "Custer State Park is a place where one can still be an unworried and unregimented individual and wear any old clothes and sit on a log and get his sanity back again." Beyond the trail and sign, hikers can climb the short distance through the boulders and reach the deadly jumping-off point.

The view from the summit (elevation 4,780 feet) is spectacular. Across the valley and in the near distance are the charred remains of the Galena Fire of 1988. Looking beyond, on clear days, hikers are treated to a view of Harney Peak, Mount Coolidge, and the Cathedral Spires.

Upon leaving Lovers' Leap, the trail descends the west side of the ridge to Galena Creek, and here hikers may experience some difficulty. The trail meanders along the narrow creekbed, and makes ten stream crossings. In dry times, crossing is easy, but in wet years the water remains high. Poison ivy abounds along the creekbed and the trail, so wear long pants and watch where you place your feet. Much of the trail is flanked with less irritating, lovelier wildflowers such as sedum, highbush cranberry, cow parsnip, Bicknell's geranium, mountain meadowsweet, bluebells, salsify, and many

Crossing a stream along Lover's Leap Trail.

prairie grasses.

After the last stream crossing, the trail leads to the road and passes by Coolidge Inn. A 10-minute walk will return you to the schoolhouse and the trailhead.

19   LEGION LAKE TRAIL

General description:	A pleasant 1.5-hour loop hike that climbs a hill on the north side of Legion Lake and offers views of the surrounding area.
Length:	1.5 miles (2.4 km).
Difficulty:	Moderate.
Trail maintenance:	Good.
Traffic:	Moderate.
Elevation gain:	400 feet.
Maps:	Trails Illustrated Topo Map No. 238; Custer State Park Trail Guide booklet, available at park office, visitor centers, and entrances.

See Map on Page 63

Finding the trailhead: From the Peter Norbeck Visitor Center, take U.S. Highway 16A west for 6 miles to Legion Lake Campground, on the right. Drive to the far end of the campground, where the trailhead is clearly marked. Park in front of the showerhouse or across the highway. Please do not block the campsites.

    0.0   Trailhead.
    0.75 Saddle is reached.
    1.1   Centennial Trail enters from north.
    1.5   Return to trailhead.

The hike: The Legion Lake Trail climbs through a ponderosa pine forest, where hikers see evidence of timber thinning and management. The summit is reached after 0.75 mile. From its rocky outcroppings, hikers can view the lake below, the Badlands to the east, and the southern Black Hills. Toward the end of the 0.75-mile descent, The Centennial Trail (see Hike 54) joins in from the north and completes the loop back to the campground.

Various species of mammals and birds use this area, including wandering bison.

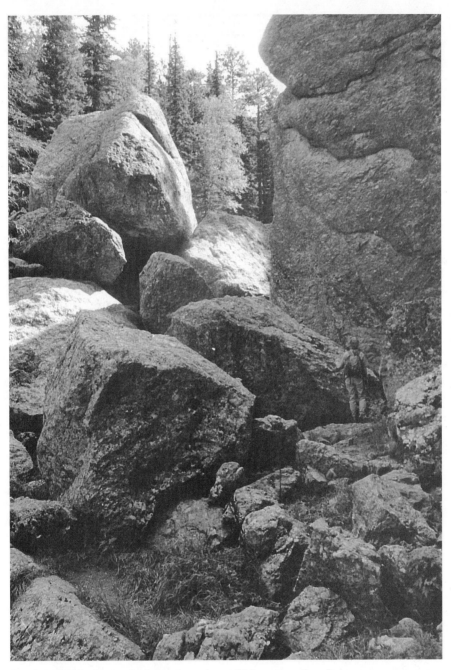

Sunday Gulch descends through an incredible maze of rocks.

General description:	An interpretive trail that loops behind Sylvan Lake and offers some of the best overviews of the park's exquisite diversity.
Length:	3.5 miles (5.6 km).
Difficulty:	Moderately strenuous.
Trail maintenance:	Fair.
Traffic:	Moderate to heavy, depending on the month.
Maps:	Trails Illustrated Topo Map No. 238; Custer State Park Trail Guide booklet, available at park office, visitor centers, and entrances.

See Map on Page 72

Finding the trailhead: From Peter Norbeck Visitor Center, take U.S. Highway 16A west, then take South Dakota Highway 87 north to Sylvan Lake, a total distance of 18.8 miles (30.2 km). Park in the day-use parking lot. Walk the Sylvan Lake Shore Trail east for 0.25 mile to the trailhead sign on the left. Or, come in at the Sylvan Lake entrance station via U.S. Highways 16/385 south from Hill City to South Dakota Highway 87 south to Sylvan Lake.

From Custer, take South Dakota Highway 89 north for approximately 7 miles to Sylvan Lake.

The hike: The Sunday Gulch Trail is considered so unique for its spectrum of plants, trees, mosses, and great scenery that it was designated a National Recreation Trail in 1971. This beautiful trail immediately descends steeply for 0.25 mile, winding over huge rocks as it drops into the depths of Sunday Gulch. The rocks can be slippery; some stone steps and handrails are provided for the first portion of the hike. Exercise caution on this part of the descent, since sometimes the handrails have been loosened over the winter by ice pushing on the railings.

As one begins the descent, huge granite walls tower on each side of the trail, which parallels the creek as it drops into the ravine. Various rock layers and formations exist here. Tiny waterfalls and rock grottos surrounded by ponderosa pine, Black Hills spruce (*picea glauca* var. *densata*), paper birch, and aspen provide photographic opportunities. Old man's beard, a gray-green lichen, hangs from the trees, adding to the mystery of the gulch. Many of the rocks are covered with mosses and lichen. Once this gulch was filled with a stream, but in the 1890s Theodor Reder dammed the mouth of the gulch and created Sylvan Lake. Today the stream spills over the dam, and at least one deep pool provides a home to brown trout.

As the trail ascends from the gulch, beautiful panoramas of the Needles formations slide into view. Toward trail's end, hikers encounter a power line, and at times the trail parallels the road; still, the beauty of the area is not diminished. The trail is well marked with orange blazes on trees.

The free interpretive guide booklet is well worth carrying, as it explains the numbered stops. Make this hike a leisurely one, allowing 3 to 4 hours.

21   PRAIRIE TRAIL

General description:	An easy interpretive loop hike through prairie grasslands and over open ridges.
Length:	3.5 miles (5.6 km).
Difficulty:	Moderate.
Trail maintenance:	Good.
Traffic:	Light.
Maps:	Trails Illustrated Topo Map No. 238; Custer State Park Trail Guide and interpretive booklet, available at park office, visitor centers, and entrance stations.

See Map on Page 63

Finding the trailhead: From the Peter Norbeck Visitor Center on U.S. Highway 16A, go east for 0.8 mile to the Wildlife Loop Road intersecting from the south. Take a right onto the Wildlife Loop Rd. and follow it for approximately 14 miles. The well-marked trailhead is on the left, with a small parking area.

From the Blue Bell entrance station on South Dakota Highway 87, take the Wildlife Loop Road southeast for 5 miles to the trailhead on the right.

The hike: The Prairie Trail was designed especially for those interested in viewing prairie grasslands and wildflowers. The interpretive brochure helps ensure more correct interpretation and adds to the enjoyment of the hike. The elevation gain is modest and climbs but 250 feet.

Views offered along this trail are commanding and, on a clear day, hikers are rewarded with distant views to the east of the White River Badlands. Even from afar, when the interplay of light and land is appropriate, the area appears majestic. So, too, does the grassland over which hikers must pass. Views of the prairie suggest an immensity and grandeur found in few other areas of the United States.

The flora is varied, and throughout the summer, pageants of flowers reward hikers. Alert travelers might also see and hear a variety of birds and mammals, such as mountain bluebirds, golden eagles, coyotes, and pronghorns.

The Prairie Trail begins by immediately crossing the narrow South Fork of Lame Johnny Creek, which, following rains, generally means wet feet. The path meanders through the grassland for a short distance, then ascends 0.25 mile along a relatively steep bluff through a stand of bur oak to a high plateau.

After breaking free from the trees, the trail follows this plateau of grasses and flowers, then descends to a fence used for bison management. The park provides a ladder up over and down the other side of the fence. From here hikers descend a short distance along the trail to where they must ford Flynn Creek, which offers an excellent example of riparian habitat.

The trail ascends again, passing through stands of bur oak, the only oak indigenous to the Black Hills. As the trail reaches the next plateau, called Hay Flats, the path winds through stands of ponderosa pine on the edge of the flats. The trail follows the plateau, passing numerous bison wallows. Soon the trail encounters another bison fence, again with a ladder provided. The fences divide the park into smaller pasturelike divisions so that the bison can be rotated among them, thus not overgrazing any one area.

About 3 miles out, the trail concludes where it began by Lame Johnny Creek.

22   BADGER CLARK HISTORIC TRAIL

General description:	A short loop trail that winds behind the historic cabin of Charles Badger Clark (1883-1957), poet laureate of South Dakota.
Length:	1 mile (1.6 km).
Difficulty:	Moderate.
Trail maintenance:	Good.
Traffic:	Moderate.
Map:	Free Custer State Park Trail Guide and interpretive booklet, available at park office, visitor centers, and entrance stations.

See Map on Page 63

Home of poet laureate Badger Clark, accessible by short trail which then progresses to command sweeping views of the Black Hills.

Finding the trailhead: From the Peter Norbeck Visitor Center, take U.S. Highway 16A west for 5.5 miles (8.85 km) to a sign on the left for the Badger Hole (Park Road 8). Follow this road for 1 mile (1.6 km) to Badger Hole Drive on the right. Turn right and go less than 0.1 mile to the trailhead parking lot.

The hike:

There's a song in the canyon below me
*   And a song in the pines overhead,*
As the sunlight crawls down from the snowline
*   And rustles the deer from his bed.*
With mountains of green all around me
*   And mountains of white up above*
And mountains of blue down the ski-line,
*   I follow the trail that I love.*
    —Badger Clark,
        The Old Prospector in Sun and Saddle Leather

This short, historic interpretive walk is great for the entire family. The trail exists because the area was once the haunt of poet Badger Clark, best known perhaps for his poem "Cowboy's Prayer." Clark lived alone for thirty years in this pristine setting, inspired by nature's bounty. He first built a one-room cabin, where he lived for ten years while building a slightly larger cabin just up the hill. An interpretive trail brochure tells more about Clark's life, and is available at the cabin and the park's visitor centers.

The trail begins with a moderate ascent through pine. At about 0.5 mile, hikers can see the charred remains of the Galena Fire of 1988 and the lookout tower atop Mount Coolidge (6,023 feet). Note the large rocks placed along the trail as it ascends to the vista. According to the interpretive brochure, this was the area where Clark originally wanted to be buried, and so he began lining the path with rocks. He often traveled this path, which provided inspiration for his work.

Custer State Park has provided ten stops along the trail, with poetry selections to be read from the brochure at each stop. Hikers should note that one of the three Centennial Trail trailheads in Custer State Park is located near this place known as the "Badger Hole" (see Hike 54).

SUNDAY GULCH TRAIL
SYLVAN LAKE SHORE TRAIL

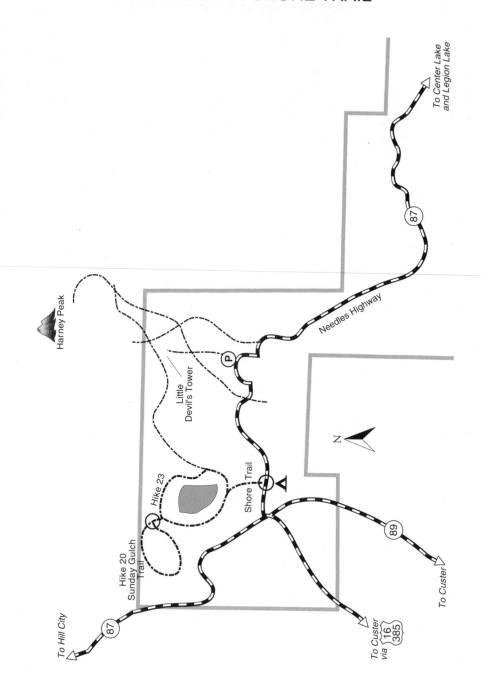

23   SYLVAN LAKE SHORE TRAIL

General description:	An easy loop trail around Sylvan Lake.
Length:	1 mile (1.6 km).
Difficulty:	Easy.
Trail maintenance:	Excellent.
Traffic:	Heavy.
Maps:	Free Custer State Park Trail Guide available at park office, visitor centers, and entrance stations.

Finding the trailhead: From Peter Norbeck Visitor Center, take U.S. Highway 16A west to South Dakota Highway 87 north (Needles Highway) to Sylvan Lake day-use area, a total of 19 miles (30.5 km).

The hike: The Sylvan Lake Shore Trail is an interpretive trail, the easiest in Custer State Park. This trail makes a loop around the lake, affording hikers wonderful views of the gigantic granite rocks in and around the lake. Interpretive signs are found at intervals, explaining the formation of the lake as well as the natural and cultural history surrounding it. This extremely easy walk is for everyone. The majority of the trail is barrier free, accessible to those in wheelchairs.

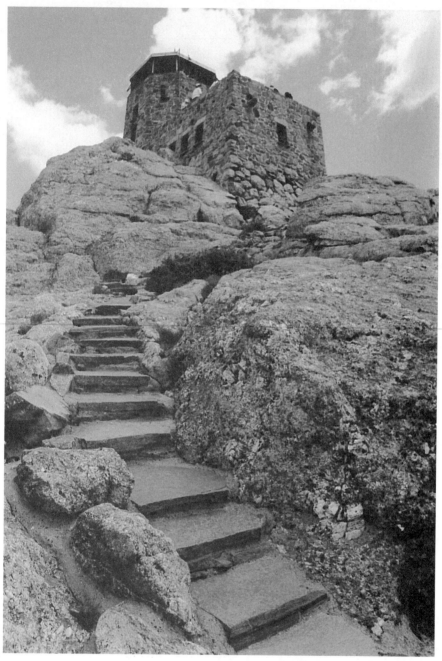

On the summit of Harney Peak steps lead to the lookout tower and provide a commanding view that sweeps out to include four states.

HARNEY RANGE

To the Lakota of the Black Hills, Harney Peak was a mythical mountain. Black Elk, a prominent medicine man among the Oglala people, considered Harney Peak the center of the world. For him, it was a place for vision quests and spiritual rejuvenation. In addition to the mountain's spiritual embodiments, Harney Peak is a significant mountain because it is the highest peak east of the main chain of the Rocky Mountains.

Harney Peak's features enchant hikers who follow trails to the peak's 7,242-foot summit. From a historic lookout tower atop the summit, hikers have distant panoramic views of South Dakota, Nebraska, Wyoming, and Montana, as well as close-up vantage points of the granite formations and cliffs of the Black Elk Wilderness.

Harney Peak was named after General William S. Harney, the commanding officer of Lieutenant G. K. Warren, who mapped the peak during a military expedition to the Black Hills in 1857. Valentine McGillycuddy also climbed the peak in the nineteenth century, completing the ascent in 1875 at the age of twenty-six. McGillycuddy mapped the peak and also photographed it. Later he served as an agent on the Pine Ridge Reservation and as the first president of the South Dakota School of Mines. When he died in 1940, his remains were cremated and placed at the base of a fire tower that had been constructed on Harney Peak. A bronze plaque is cemented in the base of the stairway to the tower containing an inscription that reads in part, "Wasicu Wakan." In Lakota, the words mean "holy white man."

The stone fire tower was constructed in 1938 and 1939 by the Civilian Conservation Corps (CCC). The CCC also constructed stone steps leading to the tower, steps that hikers still ascend today. The peak's importance for detecting fires had long been recognized. From 1911, the tower had made the life of a fire lookout here a little less extreme. In 1967, more modern techniques of spotting fires took over, and today the tower stands in mute testimony to the lonely life spotters led on the peak.

Because of its historical, geological, and spiritual significance, this 7,242-foot craggy granite peak is home to many trails. All are worth following, for each route threads through different terrain. What's more, no two days spent wandering along the peak's crest ever offer the same experience. Each season is different, too, and in years of light snowfall the trails are accessible year-round.

Three trailheads in the northwest corner of Custer State Park lead to Harney Peak: the **Sylvan Lake Trailhead**, the **Little Devils Tower Trailhead**, and the **Cathedral Spires Trailhead**. Within the Black Elk Wilderness, on the northwest fringe of Custer State Park, about 17 miles of hiking trails lead to Harney Peak from almost any direction.

NOTE: Visitors need a park entrance permit when hiking any trailheads within Custer State Park, though the Harney Range complex is managed by the Forest Service.

24 SYLVAN LAKE TRAIL

General description:	A moderately difficult trail to Harney Peak with spectacular and varied scenery along the way.
Length:	3.4 miles (5.4 km) one-way.
Difficulty:	Moderate.
Trail maintenance:	Though the trail is maintained yearly, sometimes downed trees caused by storms and buffeting winds remain on trail sections between the frequent overhauls conducted by the various trail crews.
Traffic:	Heavy at times, especially during summer. This is the main route to Harney Peak.
Elevation gain:	1,142 feet.
Highest elevation:	7,242 feet.
Maps:	Custer State Park Trail Guide, free and available at entrance stations and visitor centers; Trails Illustrated Topo Map No. 238; Black Hills National Forest Map; USGS Custer quad.

Sylvan Lake-Harney Trail

Finding the trailhead: Take South Dakota Highway 89 north from Custer for 6 miles to the Sylvan Lake entrance station. Follow signs to Sylvan Lake.

Or, from Peter Norbeck Visitor Center in Custer State Park, take U.S. Highway 16A west to South Dakota Highway 87 north (the Needles Highway) to Sylvan Lake, a distance of 19 miles (30.5 km). Access the trail from the Sylvan Lake day-use area. Follow blazes of "No. 9" on trees. The blazes are not always distinct.

0.0   Sylvan Lake–Harney Trail No. 9 trailhead.
0.75 Lost Cabin Trail enters from north. Stay on No. 9.
2.4   Intersection with Cathedral Spires Trail.
2.6   Intersection with Grizzly Bear Creek Trail. Stay on No. 9.
3.4   Harney Peak.

SYLVAN LAKE TRAIL
LITTLE DEVILS TOWER SPUR TRAIL
LITTLE DEVILS TOWER TRAILHEAD
CATHEDRAL SPIRES TRAIL

The hike: The trail provides an easy to moderate ascent for the first mile, then descends gently to the Midway Picnic Area by Lost Cabin Creek. This area has no facilities. Water from the creek should not be consumed unless purified. During the initial ascent, hikers encounter a rocky outcrop with outstanding views of Harney Peak and its surroundings.

After Midway Picnic Area, the trail ascends once more, reaching a ridge that is fairly flat. Entering the Black Elk Wilderness Area, the Cathedral Spires Trail connects from the right. About 0.25 mile later the trail is joined by Grizzly Creek Trail. Continue to follow "No. 9" blazes on trees. The final ascent of about 1 mile is steep with several switchbacks. It is flanked by stands of ponderosa pine and granite formations; in spring and summer, wildflowers abound. Close to the summit, the trail is sprinkled with mica.

Stone and mortar steps facilitate the final climb through the rocks. Group consensus proclaims the grunt to the top is worth the effort. The views of four different states rolling off and eventually merging with the horizon is inspiring. To the north, in the not-so-great distance, looms the backside of Mount Rushmore, while to the south, at a distance of about 1 mile, rugged Little Devils Tower juts to a height of 6,338 feet.

In the immediate vicinity, rock formations lace the area; the fire tower (no longer in use) straddles the most lofty of these. On clear days, the life of a fire lookout ranger could be grand, but it's easy to imagine times when winds buffeted the tower and lightning threaded the drab sky or stabbed night's inky cloak, striking the tower and engulfing it with Saint Elmo's fire.

Because of Harney Peak's grandeur, be prepared for crowds. Thunderstorms, particularly in July and August, are frequent and produce hail and lightning. At times the sun blazes, so carry plenty of water, especially in summer.

25   LITTLE DEVILS TOWER SPUR TRAIL

General description:	A fairly steep hike up a spur trail, winding through pine forest and ending atop Little Devils Tower among incredible rock formations and views.
Length:	1.5 miles (2.4 km) one-way.
Difficulty:	Moderately strenuous.
Trail maintenance:	Normally good.
Traffic:	Moderate.
Elevation gain:	300 feet.
Maximum elevation:	6,338 feet.
Maps:	Trails Illustrated Topo Map No. 238; free Custer State Park Trail Guide; Black Hills National Forest Map.

The Little Devil's Tower spur trail threads through narrow defiles.

Finding the trailhead: The trailhead is located in Little Devils Tower parking lot, which is 1 mile east of Sylvan Lake on South Dakota Highway 87 (Needles Highway). From Peter Norbeck Visitor Center in Custer State Park, take U.S. Highway 16A west to SD 87 north to Little Devils Tower parking lot on the right, a total distance of about 18 miles (28.9 km). From the east side of the parking lot, follow the trail with "No. 4" blazed on trees. A park entrance fee is required.

    0.0   Little Devils Tower Trailhead.
    0.75 Take spur trail to northeast (left).
    1.5   Little Devils Tower.

The hike: Follow Trail No. 4 and the Little Devils Tower trail east for about 0.75 mile, crossing two small streams and walking through stands of quaking aspen and Black Hills spruce. Wildflowers such as Rocky Mountain wild iris abound. At the first trail junction, hikers have a choice: the trail to the right stays on the Cathedral Spires Trail No. 4 and leads ultimately to Harney Peak. By taking the spur trail to the left, one accesses Little Devils Tower.

The spur trail begins almost immediately with a fairly steep ascent through ponderosa pine, low growing juniper and rocks that look like pancakes turned on edge and stuck in the ground. The trail then makes a sharp left turn through what appears to be a cave. But this one has no roof; the walls almost touch at the top, but not quite. The summit is reached after a steep hike of approximately 40 minutes. Follow the orange blazes on and through the lichen-covered rocks and ascend to the top of Little Devils Tower. Harney

Little Devils Tower spur trail.

Peak is directly across the narrow valley to the north and presents a wonderful display of the formations known as the Cathedral Spires. To the northeast is the backside of Mount Rushmore, and to the south hikers can view the rolling Black Hills. The panoramic view into the Black Hills central area is well worth the strenuous hike. In summer, the trail is flanked by wildflowers such as buttercups and shooting stars.

After a well-earned rest, you must now hike back down 1.5 miles to the trail junction, where you can pick up Trail No. 4 and continue on to Harney Peak (see hikes 24, 26, and 29) or save that hike for another day. Please remember that hiking off-trail in an unmarked area is not recommended or encouraged.

26   LITTLE DEVILS TOWER TRAILHEAD

See Map on Page 77

General description:	A short, pleasant walk through woods with the option of returning along the same path or connecting with the Cathedral Spires Trail to Harney Peak.
Length:	0.75 mile (1.2 km) one-way; added trails to Harney Peak make a one-way hike of 3 miles (4.8 km).
Difficulty:	Moderate to strenuous.
Trail maintenance:	Good.
Traffic:	Heavy.
Elevation gain:	1,142 feet if hikers continue on to Harney Peak.
Highest elevation:	7,242 feet (Harney Peak).
Maps:	Trails Illustrated Topo Map 238; Custer State Park Trail Guide, free at entrance stations and visitor centers; Black Hills National Forest Map.

Finding the trailhead: The trail leaves from the east end of the Little Devils Tower parking lot, which is located 1 mile east of Sylvan Lake on South Dakota Highway 87 (Needles Highway).

0.0   Trailhead.
0.75 Junction with Little Devils Tower Trail (left) or Cathedral Spires Trail (right).

The hike: This short trail, blazed with "No. 4," begins as an easy, flat ramble and continues that way for about 0.75 mile to a trail junction. This is the turnaround point for the shortest walk. If you wish to continue hiking, stay to the right at the junction; the left trail is the spur to Little Devil's Tower.

Those who wish to go on to Harney Peak should take the left-hand route.

After a 20- to 30-minute ascent through stands of ponderosa, you will connect with the Cathedral Spires Trail (No. 4), entering from the right. Follow this to Sylvan Lake Trail (No. 9), then on to Harney Peak. (See Hikes 24 and 27 for more details about the peak.)

From the west end of Little Devils Tower parking lot, you may take a short, marked trail west to Sylvan Lake.

27 CATHEDRAL SPIRES TRAIL

General description:	This moderately strenuous spur trail is a great natural history trek that connects with Sylvan Lake Trail (No. 9) to Harney Peak.
Length:	2.5 miles (4 km) one-way.
Difficulty:	Moderate to strenuous.
Trail maintenance:	Yearly.
Traffic:	Moderate to heavy.
Elevation gain:	962 feet.
Highest elevation:	7,242 feet (Harney Peak).
Maps:	Trails Illustrated Topo Map No. 238; Custer State Park Trail Guide, free and available at entrance stations and visitor centers; Black Hills National Forest Map.

> **See Map on Page 77**

Finding the trailhead: The trail is accessed from the Cathedral Spires parking lot, 2.5 miles east of Sylvan Lake on South Dakota Highway 87 (Needles Highway). You may also access it from Custer State Park's Peter Norbeck Visitor Center by taking U.S. Highway 16A west to SD 87 and going north for a total of 16.5 miles.

0.0 Cathedral Spires Trailhead at Cathedral Spires parking lot on Needles Highway.
0.5 Cathedral Spires Trail (No. 4) enters from the west from Sylvan Lake. Go northeast (right).
0.75 Norbeck Trail (No. 3) junctures from the south.
1.0 Sylvan Lake-Harney Trail (No. 9) junction. Go east on No. 9.
1.2 Grizzly Bear Creek Trail No. 7 joins from the east.
2.5 Harney Peak.

The hike: In 1977 Congress proclaimed the Cathedral Spires Trail a registered National Landmark. Limber pine—a five-needled pine tree—grows a ways in from the trail. To find this same species elsewhere, one must travel hundreds of miles north or go west to the Big Horn Mountains. Core samplings indicate that the limber pines here are hundreds of years old. The question is, how did they ever establish themselves along this remote trail deep within the Black Hills of South Dakota? Glaciologists say that, some ten thousand years ago, massive ice fields isolated these stands of *Pinus* *flexilus*. Other scientists theorize that the trees' seeds were brought into the area by bird droppings. Whatever happened, limber pine now grows along this trail as an isolated community that remains peculiar to the Black Hills.

Hikers might ponder the mystery of the pines as well as other Black Hills phenomena as they hike the beautiful and inspiring Cathedral Spires Trail. The path winds and climbs among fantastic formations that also contributed to the trail's national designation. In places these spires descend to the trail's very edges.

The Cathedral Spires Trail is a somewhat strenuous hike that begins at the east end of the parking area. At first the trail is flat, but after crossing a creek (the depth of which will depend on the rainfall of the year) it quickly begins its ascent and, with few exceptions, never stops. Watch for the number "4" blazes on trees as you make this climb through trees and rocks. Game trails lace the area and because they can at times be confused with the main trail, pay close attention to the progression of marked trees. If you lose sight of them, simply stay between the confines of the narrow valley walls until you link once again with the main trail.

Once the trail climbs through the narrow U of rock bluffs, it widens and becomes much more distinct. Devils Tower trail merges at about 0.5 mile and the two continue as one (No. 4). On top of the first saddle, projecting from about 30 feet overhead, looms what many have imagined is the figure of a robed man sculpted in rock by nature's forces. About 0.75 mile later, a sign declares you have entered the Black Elk Wilderness. In another 0.25 mile at a T intersection, the Sylvan Lake Trail No. 9 merges from the left. At this T junction, take the right-hand trail. Only 1 mile to go. (For a description of the last mile of trail to Harney Peak, see Hike 24.)

Should you decide to make this a round-trip hike returning to the Cathedral Spires parking lot, be aware that the trail becomes somewhat indistinct and could become confusing for the final mile out. Be comforted by the knowledge that should you digress from the main route and descend into a downhill gulch, you will not be the first to do so! Stay high on the ridge. Follow the trail and look carefully for tree markers. Listen for the sounds of traffic, most of which will originate from the parking lot.

Willow Creek-Sylvan Lake No.9 Trail.

28   WILLOW CREEK LOOP

General description:	An easy loop trail that provides periodic vistas of Harney Peak.
Length:	1.5 miles (2.4 km).
Difficulty:	Easy.
Trail maintenance:	Good.
Traffic:	Moderate.
Elevation gain:	100 feet.
Highest elevation:	5,200 feet.
Maps:	Trails Illustrated Topo Map No. 238; Black Hills National Forest Map; USGS Hill City and Custer quads.

Finding the trailhead: The trailhead is located at Willow Creek Horse Camp on South Dakota Highway 244, about 4 miles east of the turn off onto SD 244 from U.S. Highways 16/385. From the west, Willow Creek Horse Camp is about 4 miles west of the Mount Rushmore Memorial on SD 244 (Opposite Palmer Creek KOA).

    0.0   Trailhead, Willow Creek Horse Camp.
    1.0   Hiking southeast, encounter spur trail to Mushroom Rock.
    1.5   Completion of loop.

The hike: Willow Creek Loop Trail provides vistas of Harney Peak, a bird's-eye view of the spires of Elkhorn Mountain, and a stroll through stands of some of the Black Hills' largest ponderosa pines. Starting from Willow

WILLOW CREEK LOOP

To Lake Mt. Rushmore

Harney Trail

356.1

356.1

Sylvan Trail

Willow Creek Horse Camp

Willow Creek

Lost Cabin

Cabin Trail

357.1A

Summit Peak
5,655 ft.

357.1

Lost

Palmer Creek
Trailhead

To 87

N

1

0.5

Miles

0

To Sylvan Lake, 89

87

To Lead and
Deadwood

303.1

244

16

385

To Hill City

Creek Horse Camp one can either proceed southwest on Trails No. 2 and No. 8 or northeast on Trail No. 9. Along the way, short spur trails lead from the main trail. One short spur takes hikers to a small dam on Willow Creek. Depending on the season and the year, Willow Creek can be a full flow or a quiet seep.

About 1 mile (assuming you are proceeding in a counterclockwise direction) from the trailhead, a 600-foot-long spur trail ascends to Mushroom Rock. Here, hikers are offered views of Harney Peak and the spires of Elkhorn Mountain. Mushroom Rock is a large rock outcropping that has been sculpted by weathering into a shape that could only be named as it is.

Because the trail access is directly across the highway from a KOA campground, this loop hike provides exceptional access for KOA campers and for those camped at the Willow Creek Campground.

29   HARNEY PEAK LOOP

General description:	A series of trails through wilderness and exceptional wildlife habitat. Hikers eventually reach Harney Peak.
Length:	10.5 miles (16.9 km) round-trip.
Difficulty:	Very difficult, particularly if the entire 10.5 miles are hiked in a single day.
Trail maintenance:	Yearly. Hikers should expect to encounter blowdowns and, toward trail's end, some stream encroachment because of beaver activity.
Traffic:	Light until reaching the Sylvan Lake Trail No. 9; from Trail No. 9 to Harney Peak and back to Grizzly Bear Creek Trail, the traffic is heavy.
Elevation gain:	2,142 feet.
Highest elevation:	7,242 feet.
Maps:	Trails Illustrated Topo Map No. 238; Forest Service handout of Harney Peak Area; Black Hills National Forest Map; USGS Mount Rushmore, Iron Mountain, and Custer quads.

HARNEY PEAK LOOP

Centennial Spur Trail

Centennial

Trail

Centennial Trail

345

To 87
Custer State Park
and Wind Cave

STATE PARK

CUSTER

Iron Horse Camp
Trailhead

Creek

Bear

Trail

N

1

0.5

Miles

0

BLACK ELK WILDERNESS

Grizzly

Trail

Highway

Norbeck

Needles

87

To Hill City

U.S. Forest Service Boundary

Harney Peak
Lookout Tower

Grizzly Bear Creek Trail in Harney Ranger District.

Finding the trailhead: Although the drive to reach the trailhead begins in Custer State Park, the trailhead is just over the boundary in Black Hills National Forest. The trek begins at Iron Creek Horse Camp, where improvements are being made. To reach the trailhead, take U.S. Highway 16A west from the park's Peter Norbeck Visitor Center to South Dakota Highway 87 (Needles Highway) and go north for a total of about 7 miles. A sign on the right to Iron Creek Horse Camp indicates the next turn. Follow the dirt road about 0.5 mile, then take the first road to the left and park at the road's end.

0.0	Iron Creek Horse Camp trailhead.
2.0	Upper Iron Creek trailhead.
3.0	Sylvan Lake-Harney Trail No. 9 encountered from the west.
4.5	Harney Peak.
5.5	Grizzly Bear Creek Trail No. 7 heads east-northeast. Take this trail.
7.5	Horsethief Lake Trail joins from the north. Stay on No. 7.
9.3	Centennial Trail No. 89 comes in from the north. Stay on No. 7.
9.5	Centennial Trail No. 89 joins from the south. Take this trail.
10.5	Iron Creek Horse Camp.

The hike: For those interested in a challenging hike, this combination of four different trails provides just that. Because the distance is lengthy, some consideration should be given to camping in the Black Elk Wilderness, named for the famous Oglala medicine man who was present as a young teenager at the Battle of the Little Bighorn. Water is plentiful though it must be purified, and primitive wilderness campsites are abundant. Before pitching your tent, however, check that you are not camped in a patch of poison ivy.

The trail, heading west-southwest, begins as a dirt road at the trailhead at the end of the road on the northwest edge of the Iron Creek Horse Camp, but 0.1 mile later it becomes a more traditional trail. A short distance later the Iron Creek Trail proceeds past the cutoff to the Centennial Trail (No. 89; see Hike 54) and what will eventually be the return route from Harney Peak. Shortly thereafter the trail crosses what is often an insignificant Iron Creek, as far as stream crossings go. At this point the trail sign says "Norbeck Trail 3 and Cathedral Spires Trail No. 4."

At the beginning of the hike, much of the forest consists of bur oak, ponderosa pine, quaking aspen, and some paper birch. The bottom portion of the trail is wide but as it begins to ascend, the trail narrows and soon passes over several small saddles. About 2 miles out from the trailhead, the trail approaches and parallels the Needles Highway for about 1 mile. It then passes another possible access site, the Upper Iron Creek Trailhead.

From here the trail begins to climb abruptly to the north. Soon hikers are rewarded with close-up views of jumbled rock formations. Equally impressive are the many trees that have managed to establish footholds among these seemingly impenetrable boulders. This part of the trail passes through the west side of the Black Elk Wilderness Area.

About 3.5 miles from the Iron Creek Trailhead, hikers link with the Sylvan Lake/Harney Peak Trail No. 9, which enters from the west and continues to Harney Peak. Grizzly Bear Creek Trail No. 7 enters from the right in another 0.25 mile, and it is at this point that hikers must return from Harney Peak to begin the second leg of the loop. From this point to Harney Peak and back to Grizzly Bear Creek Trail, refer to the description in Hike 24.

After the 1.5-mile climb to Harney Peak and back, pick up the Grizzly

More than 70 miles of trails lead to Harney Peak, highest peak east of the Rockies.

Bear Creek Trail No. 7 and begin what is essentially a continuous descent. Backpackers should note that they are in the Black Elk Wilderness and that camping options are numerous, but camping is not allowed at Harney Peak or within 150 feet of a trail. Practice no-trace camping rules so that others who follow will have an equally good wilderness experience.

Because you are in a wilderness, bridges across streams are lacking. Consequently the numerous stream crossings may result in wet feet, ankles, and sometimes even thighs unless one finds a stable log or two. Vegetation on the descent is similar to what was encountered during the ascent, except for the last 3 miles. Here beaver activity is abundant and provides hikers with what certainly is one of the best examples in the Black Hills of the industriousness of this enterprising mammal. No fewer than twenty dams exist, varying in length from 75 yards to but a few feet. Beavers have modified the area's entire ecology, creating habitat upon which many other species are dependent. White-tailed deer feed on the grasses, and the impoundments created by the dams attract ducks of various species. The rushes and cattails provide prime habitat for red-winged blackbirds. About 3 miles from trail's end, the beaver impoundments often flood the trail. Count on wet boots, or include a pair of wading tennis shoes in your pack.

In another 1.5 miles, the trail converges with the Centennial Trail from the north. Continue south at this junction on Grizzly Bear Creek Trail for several hundred yards until reaching the signpost for "Centennial Trail No. 89," heading due south. Continue on this trail, which winds through rocks and woods for 1.5 miles before ending at the Iron Creek Trailhead where the hike began.

30 LOST CABIN–SYLVAN LAKE– HARNEY PEAK LOOP

General description:	A vigorous loop hike through a variety of lofty terrain so beautiful that one of the trails (Lost Cabin) has been designated a National Recreational Trail.
Length:	8.6-mile (13.8-km) loop.
Difficulty:	Strenuous.
Trail maintenance:	Seasonal. Both of these trails see horse use, so some segments are heavily eroded. When wet, these segments can be a quagmire.
Traffic:	Light to moderate, except where the trail meets the Sylvan Lake Trail 9 near Harney Peak, a heavy traffic area.
Elevation gain:	2,142 feet.
Highest elevation:	7,242 feet.
Maps:	Trails Illustrated Topo Map No. 238; free Forest Service trail handout of Harney Peak area; Black Hills National Forest Map.

LOST CABIN–SYLVAN LAKE–
HARNEY PEAK LOOP

244

To Hill City
via 16 385

Sylvan

Willow Creek
Horse Camp

To Mt. Rushmore
and Keystone

Trail

Lake

Willow

Trail

Harney

Cabin

Creek

Elkhorn Mtn.

Lost

Trail

N

0   0.5   1
Miles

Lost

Trail

Cabin

Harney

Harney Peak
Lookout

Trail

Lake

Lost   Cabin   Trail   Sylvan

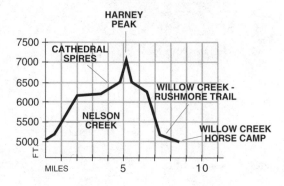

Lost Cabin Trail

Finding the trailhead: The Lost Cabin Trail trailhead is located at Willow Creek Horse Camp on South Dakota Highway 244 across from the Palmer Creek KOA, which is approximately 3 miles east off U.S. Highways 16/385 out of Custer or 4 miles west of Mount Rushmore.

0.0	Willow Creek Horse Camp trailhead.
0.75	Cross Nelson Creek.
1.00	Trail to Palmer Creek trailhead. Do not take this trail.
3.5	Junction with Sylvan Lake-Harney Trail No. 9, going east. Take this trail.
4.0	Cathedral Spires Trail No. 4 comes in from the south.
4.2	Grizzly Bear Creek Trail No. 7 comes in from the east.
5.2	Harney Peak. Descend from Harney Peak, go north on Harney Trail No. 9 toward Willow Creek Horse Camp.
7.6	Willow Creek-Rushmore Trail goes east. Continue northwest toward Willow Creek Horse Camp.
8.6	Willow Creek Horse Camp trailhead.

The hike: Part of the Harney Trail system, this hike may be one of the most picturesque in the interior. It is somewhat less strenuous if followed in the direction suggested here, but those desiring a more strenuous hike can reverse the loop. Plan to spend most of a day on this hike; you will want to stop often to absorb the views.

A trail of such immense appeal it has been designated as one of the two National Recreation Trails in the Black Hills National Forest, the Lost Cabin Trail No. 2 is quickly accessed by departing from Willow Creek Horse Camp and following the sign for "Trails 8 and 2." Immediately the Lost Cabin Trail ascends through numerous rock outcroppings and stands of ponderosa pines and birches to a saddle. At the saddle the trail begins a series of gentle ups and downs, though the general grade is up. About 0.75 mile from the trailhead take the left junction, which crosses Nelson Creek. About 0.25 mile later you will encounter a second major junction. If you take the trail to the west (right), you will shortly end up at the Palmer Creek Trailhead.

Follow Trail No. 2 south (left) and ascend to a wide saddle. At one point along the 1-mile ascent, you'll see the remains of old mining cabins. In July the trail sides are sprinkled with a variety of wildflowers. Look for camas, Indian paintbrush, harebell, and yarrow. Juniper berries weigh heavy on the low-growing bushes. At the saddle a small copse of birch graces the trail edge. To the west is a rock outcropping that provides views of Sunday Gulch and Saint Elmo's Peak.

The trail levels for a short distance then climbs moderately, entering the Norbeck Wildlife Preserve. At this point the elevation is 6,320 feet. After entering the wilderness, the trail undulates mildly, soon crossing a small stream and entering a park-like setting. In summer, bunchberry dogwood blossoms by the stream and the smell of wild mint is strong. Spire and needle formations surround the trail.

From the stream, the Lost Cabin Trail continues for another 1 to 1.25 miles where it concludes as it joins with the Sylvan Lake Trail No. 9. Hike east (left), bypassing the Cathedral Spires trail, which links with the Sylvan Lake Trail 0.3 mile after the intersection. Bypass Grizzly Creek Trail No. 7 as well, climbing another 0.75 mile until you reach the Harney Peak spur trail. Ascend the short, steep spur trail to Harney Peak.

Descend from Harney Peak and resume hiking along the Willow Creek/ Harney Peak Trail No. 9, turning left and heading north. The trail retains the designation of Willow Creek/Harney No. 9 from this point until its terminus at Willow Creek Horse Camp. This trail is mislabeled on some older Trails Illustrated maps, but the map legend is correct. The initial decent is steep. For the next mile the trail makes no fewer than 30 switchbacks as it plummets 500 feet. The trail then levels to a saddle offering superb views of Harney Peak, the backside of Mount Rushmore, and surrounding spire formations. Here, facing east, one can clearly see the Hog Back Ridge and Red Valley, which engulf the granite formations of the Central Area of the Black Hills. In the more distant east, the Badlands suggest a great mystery as they blend with the horizon.

For the next 2 miles, the trail descends and winds through ponderosa pine, eroded pinnacles and spires, and boulder fields of Elkhorn Mountain. At an intersection 2 miles before trail's end, swing northwest (left) onto a winding, old dirt road, following trail signs for Willow Creek Trailhead, where this hike concludes.

IRON MOUNTAIN LOOP

To Custer State Park

Iron Mountain Road

Creek Trail

Iron

N

Miles

0.5

1

0

Norbeck Memorial Overlook

To 16 244

Iron Mountain Trail

Iron

Centennial Bypass

Centennial

Camp Remington

345.2

To 87 Needles Highway

Centennial Trail

General description:	A loop taking hikers from mountaintop to forest floor while threading over streams, into small valleys flanked by rock formations, and through park-like settings cut by beaver dams.
Length:	5 miles (8 km).
Difficulty:	Easy to moderate.
Trail maintenance:	Good.
Traffic:	Moderate.
Elevation gain:	A 200- to 300-foot drop and gain.
Highest elevation:	5,252 feet.
Maps:	Trails Illustrated Topo Map No. 238; Black Hills National Forest Map; USGS Hill City and Custer quads.

Finding the trailhead: From the Peter Norbeck Visitor Center in Custer State Park take U.S. Highway 16A east for 1 mile. Take the left fork at the sign for Iron Mountain Road and follow that for 2 miles. Take a left onto Iron Mountain Road (US 16A) toward Mount Rushmore for 12.9 miles to the trailhead sign on the left. You are in the Peter Norbeck Wildlife Preserve, south of Mount Rushmore. The trail begins at the west end of the parking area for the Iron Mountain Picnic Area. Here restroom facilities, water, and picnic tables are available.

The Iron Mountain Trail courses through an area of mountain goat country as it approaches a saddle between rugged rock formations.

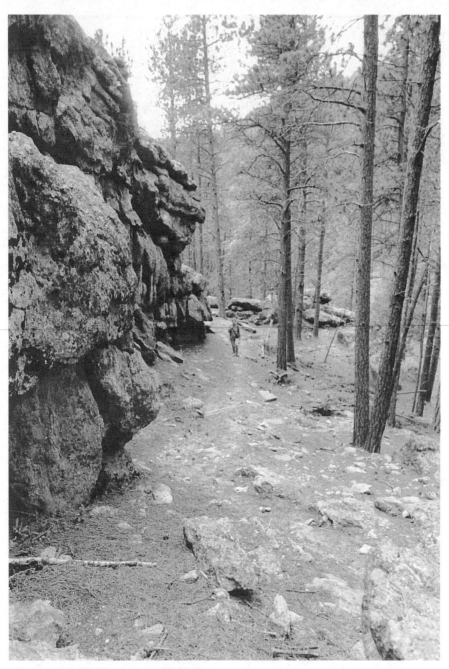

Proceeding east, the Iron Creek Trail links with the Centennial Trail, which connects with the Iron Mountain Trail.

0.0	Iron Mountain Picnic Area trailhead.
0.5	Junction with Iron Mountain Trail No. 16. Go south.
1.7	Forest Road 345.2. Head southwest (right).
2.7	Grizzly Creek Trail No. 7. Take this trail west.
3.2	Junction with Centennial Trail No. 89. Go north.
3.9	Junction with Centennial 89B to the east. Take this trail.
5.1	Iron Mountain Picnic Area trailhead.

The hike: The Iron Mountain Trail is a day trip that provides hikers with glimpses of the many facets of the Black Hills. The trail is also open in most parts to horseback riders, and the shorter 3.5-mile loop is ideal for mountain bikers, who we hope will watch for hikers on the path. Bikes are not allowed in the wilderness areas; signs are posted to that effect. The last 0.5 mile of this loop is the mountain bike bypass out of the wilderness area.

The trail begins as a wide dirt trail blazed "No. 89B." It heads west and, at 0.5 mile, joins the Iron Mountain Trail No. 16, which goes south (left). The trail is well-marked with "No. 16" blazed on trees. In this area of fascinating rock formations, look for a unique one shaped exactly like a turtle. Here, the trail appears to be an old four-wheel-drive road.

After approximately 1.2 miles, the trail meets an improved gravel road (Forest Road 345.2). Go west-southwest on the road (right). Follow the dirt road for about 1 mile, where five bridges cross Iron Creek as it meanders through the mountains. Take the next trailhead to the northwest (right), where the trail sign indicates Grizzly Creek Trail No. 7, Centennial Trail No. 89, and Harney Peak. Hiking now in a west, slightly northwest direction, you'll see inspiring rock formations. In the fall, the yellow and rust-colored leaves intermingle with the dark green of the ponderosa pine, lending even more drama to the igneous rock. Small mammals hide here, and you might catch (as we did) glimpses of an elusive mink.

After another 0.5 mile, the trail takes a hard right (the trail sign indicates Centennial Trail No. 89, Mount Rushmore, Centennial 89 Bypass) and heads north for 0.75 mile, where you'll encounter yet another junction. Follow the trail signs for 1.2 miles to the northeast (right) on 89B, thus completing the loop. This is an easy to moderate trek of 2 to 4 hours, presenting great vistas.

Another optional hike of about 4.2 miles (6.7 km) in this same area would be to begin in the same manner as described above. Upon reaching FR 345.2, however, go southeast (left) on the road for about 0.75 mile to the Iron Creek Trail No. 15. This 2-mile trail is an easy trek going due east. It follows old roads through meadows and ponderosa pine until it terminates at Lakota Lake Trailhead, adjacent to the Iron Mountain Highway. Of course, doing this one-way hike requires a shuttle between Lakota Lake and the Iron Mountain Picnic Area.

MOUNT RUSHMORE TO HORSETHIEF LAKE

32 MOUNT RUSHMORE TO HORSETHIEF LAKE

General description:	An extremely scenic one-way hike departing from Mount Rushmore and terminating at Horsethief Lake, with access to other trails, some leading to Harney Peak.
Length:	3 miles (4.8 km).
Difficulty:	Easy to moderate.
Trail maintenance:	Good.
Traffic:	Moderate.
Elevation gain:	600 feet.
Highest elevation:	5,600 feet.
Maps:	Trails Illustrated Topo Map No. 238; Black Hills National Forest Map; free Forest Service Harney Peak trails handout; USGS Mount Rushmore quad.

Finding the trailhead: The trailhead is located at the southern end of the Mount Rushmore parking lot, across South Dakota Highway 244 on the curve with a highway railing. Climb over the railing and the well-used dirt trail is easily discernible. No sign, however, points to the trailhead and we asked rangers at the entrance station to point the way.

- 0.0 Trailhead (Mount Rushmore spur trail).
- 0.2 Encounter a T intersection with Centennial Trail No. 89. Go west-northwest (right).
- 2.25 Junction with Horsethief Lake Trail No. 14 and Willow Creek-Rushmore Trail. Stay north on No. 14.
- 3.0 Horsethief Lake.

The hike: The trail markers, encountered almost immediately after winding through rocks and pine, read "No. 8," and this path will soon connect with Centennial Trail No. 89. It is the only trail leading away from Mount Rushmore, and you're only on it for about 0.25 mile, where you'll soon encounter a T intersection with Centennial Trail No. 89. Head west/northwest (to the right).

For 2 miles, the trail winds up and down through a ponderosa pine forest until another trail junction is encountered. Here you'll have several options. If continuing to Horsethief Lake, go due north (right) at this junction on trail No. 14 for about 0.75 mile into Horsethief Lake. This is a peaceful and very picturesque hike, particularly when birch and aspen leaves are turning in autumn. The trail parallels and crosses a stream with several small, beautiful waterfalls. Granite rock formations rise steeply on each side, giving the sensation of entering an area known by no one else.

The other options at the trail junction mentioned above are as follows: Follow Horsethief Lake Trail No. 14 south (left) for 2 miles to the junction

Several trails in the Harney Range depart from Mount Rushmore. Others provide periodic views of the faces carved by Gutzon Borglum.

with Grizzly Bear Creek Trail No. 7. An easy to moderate walk, this route offers hikers magnificent views of the entire Harney Peak area as it ambles through lofty peaks and spires. According to the free Forest Service trail handout, excellent backpack camping sites exist here, especially on the saddles that are a moderate climb off the trail. The Horsethief Lake Trail ends at this point, and Grizzly Bear Creek Trail No. 7 joins the trail.

To make a loop from this point back to Mount Rushmore, take Grizzly Bear Creek Trail No. 7 southeast (left) for 1.5 to 2 miles. This is a hike of moderate descent that is partly a trail and partly an old four-wheel-drive road passing through meadows and past beaver ponds flanked by rock wall formations. The trail continues uninterrupted until Centennial Trail No. 89 joins from the north. Take this trail north for slightly more than 3 miles, following signs for Mount Rushmore. The ascent is moderate as the trail passes through pine forests and unique rocks, offering views of the surrounding peaks. The Mount Rushmore spur trail enters from the northeast (right); take that for 0.25 mile to SD 244 and the parking lot at Mount Rushmore.

To access Harney Peak from the point where the Horsethief Lake Trail ends, take Grizzly Bear Creek Trail No. 7 west/northwest. This 2.25-mile hike is strenuous as it ascends 1,000 feet in the final 1.5 miles. A lightly used trail, the route brings hikers to the solitude and peace of the Black Elk Wilderness. As the Grizzly Bear Creek Trail ends, hikers should take the Sylvan Lake Trail No. 9 to the summit of Harney Peak, about 1 mile farther.

DEERFIELD/PACTOLA

OVERVIEW

In 1874, two years before the infamous battle along Montana's Little Bighorn River, General George A. Custer led his U.S. Army troops into the Black Hills. Custer was looking for a site that might be appropriate for constructing a fort. Accordingly, a cartographer traveled with the Seventh Cavalry and helped map much of the Black Hills. With this information, settlers soon followed, since the Custer Expedition also helped secure the area against Indians determined to defend the integrity of the Paha Sapa. These were their spiritual grounds, and a place where many traveled in search of vision quests. The discovery of gold changed all that. Though the Black Hills were promised by treaty to the Lakota, the lure of gold was too great, and the promises were broken. The fate of the Native Americans in the Black Hills was sealed.

During the 1874 expedition, Custer and his men camped on Castle Creek at what eventually became known as Deerfield (first known as Mountain City). Deerfield was the site of a brief gold rush, and a small town evolved there and remained until 1940, at which time developers moved the store, school, post office, and other buildings to make way for the impoundment resulting from construction of Deerfield Dam.

About the same time Deerfield emerged, other mining towns also evolved, and several still linger along the route traversed by the Deerfield Trail. Canyon City, just below the mouth of Slate Creek, took root between the 1880s and 1890s, when men worked placer mines here. Silver City, near trail's end, was once home to three hundred people, many of whom dug for gold, silver, antimony, and mercury. Today only a few residents remain.

The Silver City Trailhead is located at the end of town on Rapid Creek, a great trout-fishing stream. The Deerfield Trail, completed in 1992, and its associated Lake Loop Trail expose a slice of history unique to the Black Hills.

The Deerfield Trail also approaches three other towns that at one time hummed with activity and the thud and pound of dredge, ax, and shovel. Two of these are Castleton and Mystic. Though the townsite of Castleton has faded with time, Mystic retains a number of its structures. As a result of its history, much of the small village has been placed on the National Register of Historic Places. Mystic was first named Sitting Bull by miners in 1876. As the town developed and the mining activity flourished, railroad tracks were laid. These carried trains as recently as 1983. One of the town's most long-lived operations was a sawmill, which provided jobs for other residents and which operated until 1952. Today, the George S. Mickelson Trail (Hike 55) links with the Deerfield Trail near the Mystic Trailhead and directs trail users to Mystic, less than a mile away. The Deerfield Trail and the George Mickelson Trail are sometimes one and the same.

Hikers and bikers often follow the old Grand Island & Wyoming Central

Railroad (later the Burlington Northern) rail lines. Those who hike to Castleton and Mystic are traveling along this old rail line. As well as slicing through much of the nation's mining and railroad history and South Dakota's in particular, the Deerfield Trail provides access to some of the state's best fishing. Deerfield Lake offers anglers the opportunity to catch rainbow trout. The more eastern portions of the trail provide access to brown trout fisheries. One eastern portion of the trail is a designated walk-in fishery and excludes all motorized vehicle use. The Deerfield Trail passes through some of the most spectacular country in the Black Hills, an area abundant with wildlife. Look to the meadows for white-tailed deer, to the streams for beaver, and the woods for turkey.

One Forest Service ranger who has hiked the Deerfield Trail on a number of occasions suggests making the trek a three-day one, camping out two nights. One suggested campsite is about 1 mile west of the Mystic Trailhead; another is along Rapid Creek, about 2 miles west of the Silver City Trailhead. Because the elevation loss is about 1,600 feet as one travels west to east, we recommend that you proceed in that direction.

Hill City, South Dakota, "The Heart of the Hills," may be used as the

DEERFIELD/PACTOLA

jumping-off place for roads to the various Deerfield/Pactola trails. Hill City is about 28 miles (45 km) southwest of Rapid City on U.S. Highway 16W. To reach Hill City from Custer, take U.S. Highways 385 and 16 north for 14 miles.

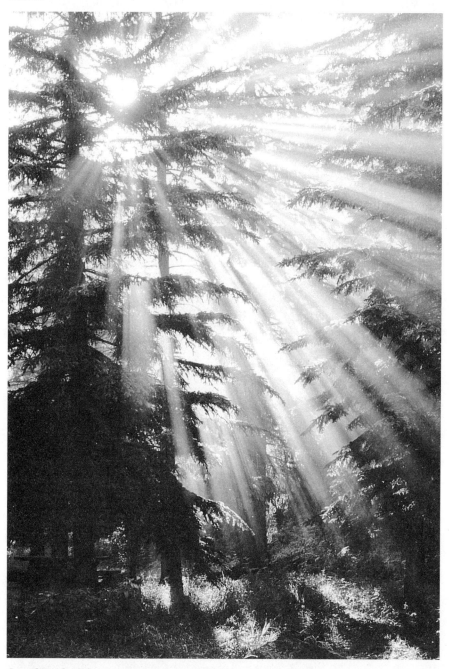

Sun-drenched forest along the Deerfield Trail.

General description:	Suitable for both hikers and mountain bikers, the Deerfield Trail slices through segments of the nation's history and some of the Black Hills' more pristine country.
Length:	18 miles (28.9 km) one-way.
Difficulty:	Moderate to difficult.
Trail maintenance:	Yearly.
Traffic:	Light to moderate.
Elevation gain:	Moderate if traveling west to east; 1,600 feet if traveling east to west.
Highest elevation:	Signal Knob, 6,200 feet.
Maps:	Black Hills National Forest Map, available at Forest Service offices and visitor centers; USDA Forest Service Map No. 40, free from Forest Service offices and Black Hills visitor centers.

Deerfield Trail

Finding the trailheads: To reach the **Custer Trailhead** and Deerfield Lake, follow Forest Road 17 (also called Deerfield Road) northwest out of the center of Hill City for 20 miles until it intersects with Forest Road 417. Follow FR 417 for 2 miles to Deerfield Lake and the Custer Trailhead, a total of 22 miles from Hill City. The Custer Trailhead is common to both the Deerfield Trail (40) and Deerfield Lake Loop Trail (40L).

To begin at the **Kinny Canyon Trailhead**, start in Hill City and proceed 10 miles along FR 17 until it intersects with Forest Road 188 (also called Slate Prairie Road). Turn right at the fork and proceed 8 miles to the trailhead.

The **Mystic City Trailhead** can also be reached from Hill City. Take FR 17 northwest for 5 miles until it intersects with Forest Road 231. Go 5.9 miles to the Mystic Trailhead, on the left.

Take US 385 north from Hill City for 18 miles until it intersects with FR 321. Follow this road 0.25 mile to the **Deer Creek Trailhead**. This trailhead is common to both the Deerfield Trail and the Centennial Trail (Hike 54).

DEERFIELD TRAIL

DEERFIELD TRAIL

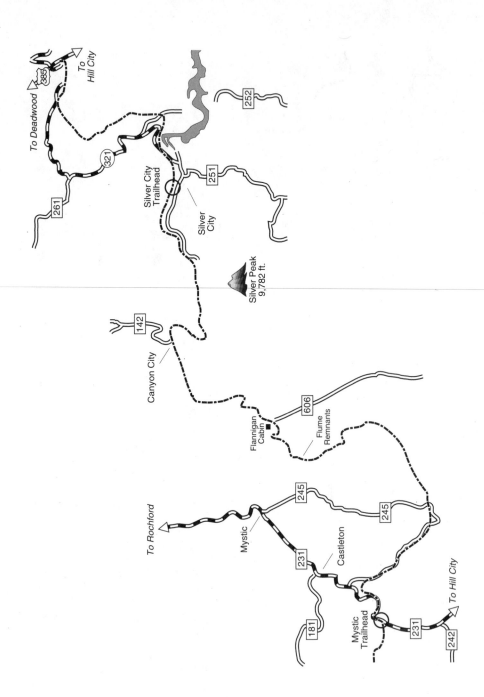

To get to the **Silver City Trailhead**, take US 385 north from Hill City for 18 miles to sign for Silver City. Turn left and continue on Forest Road 321 for 5 miles to the trailhead, a total of 23 miles.

The hike description below starts at the Custer Trailhead.

0.0   Custer Trailhead.
2.0   Signal Knob.
7.0   Mystic Trailhead.
14.0   Rapid Creek.
15.5   Silver City.
18.0   Deer Creek Trailhead.

The hike: Completed in 1992, the Deerfield Trail is one of the Black Hills' most recent additions. Because elevation loss (or gain) along the route is substantial, the trail's entire 18 miles is most easily traveled by proceeding from west to east.

From the Custer Trailhead at Deerfield Lake, the Deerfield Trail's western terminus, the trail ascends and descends for about 2 miles through Reynolds Prairie, high above the lake. It then passes the Kinny Canyon Trailhead at mile 3, concluding its climb at Slate Prairie and nearby Signal Knob, which at an elevation of 6,200 feet is the highest point along the Deerfield Trail. Here, the trail passes through a gate as the vegetation changes from ponderosa to a prairie ecosystem. Deer often graze in the meadows of Slate Prairie, and it's worth pausing to examine the grassy swales for movement.

The trail crosses a road 0.1 mile later and offers a brief view of Harney Peak, some 14 miles to the southeast. The trail then descends to a small creek and reenters the forest, which in places has been recently logged. The trail then climbs once again, though its general trend is always down.

Gen. George Custer and his men camped on Castle Creek at what eventually became known as Whitetail Gulch. The trail parallels Crooked Creek—flanked by stands of quaking aspen—where it soon intersects with the spur from the Mystic Trailhead. Just north are the Castleton dredge mining sites and Mystic, a mining camp turned railroad town. To the south is the old Mystic Civilian Conservation Corps camp, active in the 1930s.

At the Mystic Trailhead, the trail crosses FR 231 and follows it for about 0.25 mile to the George Mickelson Trail (Hike 55), now under construction. The Deerfield Trail then veers from the Mickelson Trail and climbs a four-wheel-drive trace, passes through a fence, and continues ascending through a stand of aspen until, at last, it crests.

The trail then drops through Lind Gulch. Here the vegetation changes to ponderosa and soon enters the sheer-walled canyon of Slate Creek Canyon, through which the trail passes for almost 3 miles. The entire trail to this point has been ideal for both hikers and mountain bikes, but this is one 1-mile stretch where hiking is much preferred. Cyclists must carry their bikes over rocks and, in one place, hoist them up rock outcroppings. Although the Forest Service has placed more than thirty flattened-log bridges here, high water takes its toll, forcing travelers to sometimes wade. (Other than a few segments of the trail in Slate Creek Canyon, the trail is appropriate for both hikers and cyclists, the latter of whom seem to dominate. Cyclists should remember when descending to maintain control, not only for their own safety but for that of slower hikers as well.)

In addition to being an extraordinarily beautiful canyon, Slate Creek serves as a prime fishery. Hikers would do well to pack a tent and fishing rod and spend several hours or days matching wits with the elusive brown trout here. When not involved in quality angling, history buffs will enjoy investigating the background of deteriorating cabins. As you travel, you'll pass Black Tom Mine, Flannigan Cabin, and the Warren-Lamb flume, which in 1920 carried logs to the Canyon City railhead. Despite time, some of these structures remain in exceptional condition, and the Forest Service asks travelers to leave them as they find them.

About 6 miles beyond the Mystic Trailhead, Slate Creek converges with Castle Creek, and the two are redesignated Rapid Creek. From this point to the Silver City Trailhead the going is fairly easy. By now the Deerfield Trail has descended to just over 4,600 feet and it is broad and flat. Bridges here are planked and broad for greater crossing ease. Fishing in some of the rocky canyons and their deep holes along Rapid Creek is excellent. The Forest Service has designated the segment as a walk-in fishery only.

Once this portion of the trail was traversed by the Rapid City, Black Hills & Western railway, which crossed more than a hundred bridges on its way to Mystic. The rails have been removed, making the segment of the trail along Rapid Creek to Silver City ideal for hikers, cyclists, and cross-country skiers.

From the Silver City Trailhead, the canyon widens and begins a 2.5-mile climb. Finally the Deerfield Trail links up with the Centennial Trail at the Deer Creek Trailhead, some 18 miles from where it originated.

34 DEERFIELD LAKE LOOP

General description:	A winding loop trail that begins in a prairie and meanders through ponderosa pine forests as it circles Deerfield Lake.
Length:	10-mile (16-km) loop.
Difficulty:	Moderate to strenuous.
Trail maintenance:	Yearly.
Traffic:	Light.
Elevation gain:	400 feet.
Highest elevation:	6,220 feet.
Maps:	Black Hills National Forest Map, available for purchase at Forest Service offices and visitor centers; Forest Service Maps No. 40 and 40L, free from Forest Service offices and visitor centers.

Finding the trailhead: To access the Custer Trailhead on the north shore of Deerfield Lake, proceed west from Hill City on Forest Road 17 (Deerfield Road) for 20 miles until the road intersects with Forest Road 417. Follow FR 417 several miles to the sign for Custer Campground. The Lake Loop can also be accessed from the North Shore Trailhead on the northwest end of FR 17 and FR 461; from the Hilltop Trailhead on the southern side of the lake; and from the Goldrun Trailhead, 1 mile east of Hilltop Trailhead on FR 17.

    0.0   Custer Trailhead at Custer Campground.
    1.5   Trail to Deerfield Dam.
    3.75 Cross paved FR 17.
    6.5   Castle Creek footbridge.
  10.0   Loop ends on road just outside Custer Campground.

The hike: We began by hiking clockwise from the Custer Trailhead at the Custer Campground (also the western terminus of Deerfield Trail No. 40). The somewhat rocky trail begins as a progression of sharp, short ascents and descents through the southern end of Reynolds Prairie, passing

DEERFIELD LAKE LOOP

through three cattle gates. In summer, a variety of wildflowers bloom. Because this is a multiple-use area, many gates are encountered throughout the hike. Be sure to leave them as they are, open or closed.

For the next 1.5 miles you follow both Trails 40 and 40L, and symbols for both routes are displayed. Signs shaped like deer prints signify Deerfield Trail 40; signs showing a lake engulfed by undulating waves signifies Deerfield Lake Loop 40L in the open areas. In wooded areas, follow the gray diamonds nailed on trees for the Lake Loop Trail.

Approximately 1.5 miles from the trailhead, descend steeply onto a dirt road. Here you have the option of detouring for a short side trip to the right for 0.25 mile to the top of Deerfield Dam, banked 171 feet above the level of nearby Castle Creek streambed. Back on the trail and three narrow, ankle-deep stream crossings later, you will reach the junction of trails 40 and 40L. Take 40L, which juts to the right, heading south.

Until this point lake views are numerous, but from here, those vistas become fewer as the trail begins to progress in a somewhat constant series of ups and downs through the ponderosa pine forest. Quiet and lucky hikers often catch views of wildlife amidst the huge trees. About 3 miles into the hike, the trail crosses directly over a dirt road, Forest Road 607. The narrow path swings west, still in the forest. About 0.75 mile later, after a steep descent offering a great lake view (near Gold Run Trailhead), cross FR 17 to the south side, directly opposite a private campground. Go through the gate (you might have to crawl over or under) to pick up the trail, which then parallels the highway for about 2 miles, heading west. Hilltop Trailhead is located here on the north side of the highway.

Following the signs, you must then cross back over FR 17 where a small footbridge takes you over Castle Creek. The fishing here is supposed to be good. The final 2.5 to 3 miles assume a series of steep ups and downs around the northwest side of the lake, winding high on dirt cliffs and passing through woods and open fields until the trail concludes on the gravel road just outside Custer Campground.

General description:	A fascinating trek through one of the historic gold-mining areas in the Black Hills. The trail follows, in part, an old flume bed.
Length:	11 miles (17.7 km) one-way, with optional 3-mile addition (see Hike 36).
Difficulty:	Easy to moderate.
Trail maintenance:	Yearly, with good interpretive descriptions throughout.
Traffic:	Light to moderate.
Elevation gain:	900 feet.
Highest elevation:	5,300 feet.
Maps:	Black Hills National Forest Map, available for purchase at Forest Service offices and at visitor centers; USDA Forest Service Flume Trail No. 50 map, free at Forest Service offices and Black Hills visitor centers.

> **See Map on Page 114**

Flume Trail

Finding the trailhead: Take U.S. Highway 385 north from the center of Hill City for 6 miles to Sheridan Lake Campground on the right. Go through the entrance gate and follow the signs for the Flume Trail and Centennial Trail trailheads on the southeast shore of the lake. This is the western terminus of the Flume Trail and is called the Calumet Trailhead. The eastern terminus, Coon Hollow Trailhead, is 0.25 mile from the old mining town of Rockerville, located on Forest Road 233, which is about 16 miles northeast of Hill City off U.S. Highway 16 east.

0.0	Western terminus, Calumet Trailhead.
1.0	Centennial Trail No. 89 junction. Do not follow.
2.0	First tunnel.
2.2	Second tunnel.
3.0	Baker Meadow overlook.
7.0	Boulder Hill Trailhead. Also location of Spring Creek Loop Trail and Boulder Hill.
11.0	Eastern terminus, Coon Hollow Trailhead.

Old flume bed, along Flume Trail.

The hike: The Flume Trail is filled with the history of gold mining of the area and is, in addition, a wonderful nature walk. One of two National Recreation Trails in Black Hills National Forest, the path follows much of an old flume bed. Old parts of the wooden flume can still be seen along this route, as can other historic artifacts. Many photographic opportunities exist on this trail, including canyons, forests, tunnels, and prairie fields alive with wildflowers in summer. The trail treks through the history of gold mining, and hikers can't help but recall the miners who built the flume with picks, hammers, and shovels.

Hike this trail in one day or make it a comfortable two-day hike. Camp anywhere as long as the campsite is at least 100 feet off the nearest trail or road. Those desiring to hike the entire length of trail one-way should arrange for a shuttle. Those wishing to backtrack or hike shorter segments can access the trail from two other trailheads, the Upper Spring Creek Trailhead (about 1 mile east of Calumet Trailhead), or the Boulder Hill Trailhead (about 2.75 miles from the trail's eastern terminus).

From the parking lot at Sheridan Lake, the trail begins by crossing a small footbridge over a clear feeder creek. Flume Trail No. 50 shares this easy, relatively flat walk with Centennial Trail No. 89 for about 1 mile. Together they parallel the lakeshore as they head toward the east end of the lake and the earthen dam. Upon reaching the dam, No. 89 heads north; about 20 feet prior to that, the Flume Trail No. 50 cuts sharply to the east (right) into pine forest. The trail markers on brown posts are a distinctive red, white, and blue, signifying a National Recreation Trail. At this first junction, hikers ascend to the ridge above the dam.

Beginning mile 2, the path ascends and descends briefly in a small series of switchbacks through the ponderosa woods. Soon you encounter the first of many signs along the trail that interpret the Rockerville Flume, vital to the area's gold mining operations in the late 1800s. The path then ascends out of Blue Lead Draw to Spring Creek Canyon. The creek can be heard 140 feet below as it rushes into the lake.

Continue walking along a cliff base above a boulder field, for about 1.5 miles in from the trailhead where you'll reach the first of two old tunnels on the trail. Very low and cut entirely by hand and back muscle into ancient rock, this tunnel extends for 75 to 100 feet. If you have an aversion to dark, low places have the option of hiking over the top. The trail then begins to swing away from the canyon. At the next interpretive sign you have the option of going north (right) to the Upper Spring Creek Trailhead (which is also a walk-in fishing area) or continuing straight on the Flume Trail.

Continuing on the Flume Trail, the second tunnel is soon reached, this one about 25 feet long. The trail then swings due south for 0.5 mile, descends to cross a feeder creek, then ascends gently to the north. At this point you will pick up the first of many old four-wheel-drive trails that the Flume Trail follows. Ascend through a flower-strewn meadow to the Baker Park overview, which offers a prime example of a prairie and forest edging. An "edge" is an ecological term indicating an area wildlife prefer because of the juxtaposition of food and cover.

FLUME TRAIL
SPRING CREEK LOOP
BOULDER HILL

At this point you are 4.25 miles west of Boulder Hill, and this massive rocky hill (elevation 5,331 feet) can easily be seen to the east on clear days. The trail makes another series of gently rolling descents and ascents in meadows and woods, on and off old four-wheel-drive roads. Until this point the trail has been well marked, but 1.5 miles west of Boulder Hill Trailhead it can become confusing. Trail markers are often absent, but some "Foot Travel Only" signs exist. Follow these as the trail heads north for 0.75 mile then swings southeast for another 0.75 mile, at which point it crosses then parallels Forest Road 358 and leads to the Boulder Hill Trailhead parking lot.

At this trailhead, you have the option of taking an extra half-hour hike to the top of Boulder Hill (leave time to linger there) and/or hike the easy 3-mile (4.8-km) Spring Creek Loop Trail (see Hike 36), before completing the last few miles of the Flume Trail. Leaving Boulder Hill the trail proceeds east and slightly southeast, following the trail markers and "Foot Travel Only" signs. For the first mile or so you may have to search out the signs a bit, but the final 2 miles to Coon Hollow Trailhead are well marked and have interpretive signs along the way.

The trail is broader toward the end as it winds through the forests. Pass over a rock cut through which the flume water flowed, dug by hand. One of the last interpretive signs informs travelers that they've reached the downstream terminus of the flume. Upon reaching Coon Hollow Trailhead, (the eastern terminus of the Flume Trail), the town of Rockerville (population 20) is about 0.75 mile west.

36 SPRING CREEK LOOP

General description:	A flat loop trail through woods on a ridge above Spring Creek, which can be included as an addition to the Flume Trail (Hike 35) or simply hiked on its own.
Length:	3-mile (4.8-km) loop.
Difficulty:	Easy.
Trail maintenance:	Good to fair.
Traffic:	Light.
Maps:	Black Hills National Forest Map, available for purchase at Forest Service offices and at visitor centers; USDA Forest Service Map No. 50 (Flume Trail), free at Forest Service offices and Black Hills visitor centers.

> **See Map on Page 114**

Finding the trailhead: Spring Creek Loop Trail is accessed from the Boulder Hill Trailhead, considered the mid-section of the Flume Trail. From Hill City take U.S. Highway 16 east for 11.1 miles to Forest Road 358 on the left of the highway. Follow this dirt road for 2.3 miles to the trailhead.

0.0	Boulder Hill Trailhead.
1.0	Interpretive sign.
2.5	Cross Forest Road 385.
2.7	Cross back over FR 385.
3.0	Boulder Hill Trailhead.

The hike: Part of the Flume Creek National Recreation Trail, Spring Creek Loop Trail is marked by the distinctive red, white, and blue NRT markers on posts for the first 2 miles. The path is marked for foot travel only.

From the trailhead parking lot we hiked counterclockwise, following the sign for Spring Creek Loop to the north. Immediately the trail parallels an old road that is obviously intended to be returned to a natural condition and passes huge piles of old wood. A comfortable, wide, forest path, the Spring Creek Loop Trail meanders along a cliff edge and through stands of ponderosa pine.

At about 1 mile, an interpretive sign informs you that you're standing on an old flume bed, 300 feet above Spring Creek. Spring Creek is a great trout stream, but too difficult to reach from this trail. There are other access sites, such as Spring Creek Canyon, below Sheridan Lake. Parallel the creek—which you hear more than you see—for another 0.5 mile. The trail then begins to wind south.

Hike an other 0.5 mile and you'll see rocky and woody remnants of the old flume. But here the trail can become a bit indistinct. Continue walking south, following signs that say "Foot Travel Only," and you will soon cross the dirt FR 385. The trail parallels the road for several hundred yards, crosses FR 385 once more, then returns to the trailhead.

37 BOULDER HILL

General description:	A short but steep ascent (a 20- to 30-minute hike) to the top of a high, rocky outcropping, offering dramatic views.
Length:	1 mile, one-way.
Difficulty:	Strenuous.
Trail maintenance:	Yearly.
Traffic:	Light.
Elevation gain:	400 feet in a short distance.
Highest elevation:	5,331 feet.
Maps:	Free Forest Service brochure of Flume Trail (FS No. 50); Black Hills National Forest map.

See Map on Page 114

Finding the trailhead: Boulder Hill is accessed from the Boulder Hill Trailhead along the Flume Trail (see Hike 36).

The hike: Boulder Hill is one of the special features found along the Flume Trail and makes another nice side trip on the Flume Trail hike—or a good jaunt just for its own sake. Located south of Spring Creek Loop and Boulder Hill Trailhead, this short, steep, spur hike is well worth the effort. Upon reaching the 5,331-foot summit, we agreed that it would be a perfect vision quest spot, in addition to being a photographer's dream.

A marker adjacent to the Spring Creek Loop Trail points the way around the base of Boulder Hill to the east side, where a narrow trail then ascends quite steeply for several hundred feet through the craggy rocks to the summit. Hikers can alternately locate the primitive old road on the west side and take that up—we found the old road rather difficult to follow, so we opted for the marked trail. Because forest roads surround Boulder Hill, getting lost is difficult—so plain bushwhacking is also an option.

From the peak, the sensational 360-degree vistas include the Badlands, rolling prairies, the Needles formations, and Harney Peak.

General description: Two high-mountain loop trails affording hikers and mountain bikers extraordinary views and a great diversity of vegetation and wildlife.

Length: 16.1 miles (25.9 km) for the combined loops. Trail 25 is 6.5 miles (10.4 km), including the spur trail; Trail 23 is 9.1 miles (14.9 km) with an optional 0.4-mile spur.

Difficulty: Easy to moderately strenuous.

Trail maintenance: Yearly.

Traffic: Light.

Elevation gain: 1,300 feet.

Highest elevation: 7,153 feet.

Maps: Black Hills National Forest Map, available for purchase at Forest Service offices and visitor centers; USDA Forest Service Map of Bear Mountain Trails No. 23 and 25, free at Forest Service offices and Black Hills visitor centers.

Bear Mountain Ski Trails

Finding the trailhead: The trails are accessed from Medicine Mountain Boy Scout Camp, which is located west of Hill City and northwest of the town of Custer. Signs for the camp are found on U.S. Highway 16, pointing you in the right direction. From Custer, SD, proceed as follows: take U.S. Highways 385/16 north from Custer for about 4 miles. Take County Road 297 northwest for about 8 miles, then follow Forest Road 299 (Bobcat Road) north for 3 to 4 miles to the Boy Scout Camp.

0.0	Medicine Mountain Boy Scout Camp.
2.0	Bear Mountain Fire Lookout.
4.0	Spur Trail to Grand Vista.
5.7	End of Trail 25.
9.0	Medicine Mountain Boy Scout Camp.

The hike: The Forest Service is justifiably proud of the Bear Mountain

Ski Trails and hopes they will be used more frequently by hikers and mountain bikers. Bear Mountain is one of the highest mountains in the Black Hills at 7,153 feet. At its peak is a fire tower, one of the principal towers in the area. For hikers on Bear Mountain trails, the 400-yard spur off Trail 25 to the lookout offers views that are breathtaking. The other vantage point at the Grand Vista Overlook (7,040 feet) is equally spectacular, offering views of Harney Peak, Little Devils Tower, the Cathedral Spires, and many other landmarks. This overlook is also on a spur trail off Trail 25.

Certainly one of the best reasons to hike these trails is the varied scenery. The trails wind through draws, pass through pine and spruce forests, skirt stands of aspen, and travel along a limestone rim. Wildlife is abundant in this area. According to Bear Mountain trail personnel, mountain lions occasionally are seen. Elk and deer abound; coyotes, grouse, and wild turkeys are sometimes glimpsed.

The Medicine Mountain Boy Scout Camp serves as the trailhead for both trails. It's perfectly all right to park overnight there, and restroom facilities are available. Trail 25 is 6.5 miles (10.4 km) long, including the spur trail. Trail 23 is 9.1 miles (14.9 km) long with an optional 0.4-mile spur.

BEAR MOUNTAIN SKI TRAILS

Beginning on the southern route of Trail 25, hikers ascend 1,000 feet in about 2 miles to Bear Mountain. If you want to visit the fire tower, the spur trail here is only 0.5 mile. Return to Trail 25 and follow the limestone rim to the spur Trail 25A, which heads northeast for 0.8 mile to the Grand Vista Overlook. The name says it all; from here you can see more than thirty mountain peaks.

BEAR MOUNTAIN SKI TRAILS (DETAIL)

Return to Trail 25 and head northwest down Grand Vista Draw. Trail 25 concludes 5.7 miles from here, at the intersection with Trail 23. By heading east on Trail 23, you can make a loop, traveling down Spring Creek and returning to the trailhead from which you started. For a very long hike, you can continue north on Trail 23 up Long Draw. By doing this you follow the perimeter of the loop trails, making a one- or two-day hike of some 16 miles.

Our trail profile delineates Trail 25 and Trail 23, combining to make the shorter loop of the two. The trails are well marked by signs with a bear claw in a square indicating the ski trail. In densely wooded areas, blue diamond blazes are used.

The free trail brochure available from the Forest Service notes segments of both trails that are used by snowmobilers during the winter season. Drinking water is not available on the trails. Be sure to purify any stream or spring water you use.

ADDITIONAL TRAILS

Veterans Point

Hikers who seek views and easy walking can take the barrier-free, 0.5-mile (0.8-km) Veterans Point trail around a point overlooking Pactola Reservoir. The paved walk at Veterans Point is open year-round. There is also a short one-way spur trail of 1,200 feet off the loop. The grade on the trail is 6 percent, which can be somewhat challenging for visitors in wheelchairs. There are curbs and railings along the trail, however. The path loops around a point, offering wonderful views of Pactola Reservoir, the rocky shoreline, and the hills surrounding the area.

To reach the trailhead from Hill City, take U.S. Highway 385 north for approximately 16 miles to Pactola Visitor Center on Pactola Reservoir. The Veterans Point walk is located about 1 mile north of the visitor center on US 385 at the northeast end of the reservoir and the dam.

Aspen Leaf

Another short (0.25-mile) interpretive trail is located at the Pactola Visitor Center. The first portion of the Aspen Leaf Trail is barrier-free, but the trail ranges from easy to strenuous. This interpretive trail was designed to show and identify several regional species of plants and trees. The trail begins as a paved observation sidewalk that goes around the back side of the visitor center, offering great views of Pactola Reservoir. This portion of the walk is barrier-free with a 5 percent slope. The trail then leads downhill on a series of steps to an observation deck. From here, walkers can proceed downhill even farther, to the edge of the reservoir.

The trail begins and ends at the Pactola Visitor Center on Pactola Reservoir, 16 miles north of Hill City on U.S. Highway 385.

WIND CAVE NATIONAL PARK

OVERVIEW

Late one July afternoon we sat on Boland Ridge looking west over a broad expanse of land known as Red Valley. Below us in the distance, large black dots quickly assumed the distinct and recognizable forms of bison. Mating season was at its height, and several of the bulls had not yet determined their order of dominance. They were angry and were fighting in earnest.

Raising our binoculars, we watched as two gigantic bulls galloped side by side. Suddenly one of them stopped and wheeled. The two collided, but with no apparent ill affect. Red dust rose around the two, and they began raking one another with their daggerlike horns. Within a minute, the battle was over. Just what these two giants had concluded was unclear, but for no apparent reason the fighting ceased and the two began grazing in the tall prairie grasses, seemingly oblivious to one another.

We sat on the ridge watching for more than an hour as similar battles continued. The setting was a primordial one, a scene from prehistoric times. Then, with little warning, a violent afternoon storm blew in. For 10 minutes wind, rain, and hail assaulted us. When it ended, only the hushed breath of the prairie breeze stirred the grasses. Not a single bison dotted the landscape, and the silence was immense. Seldom had we been more moved by such immense beauty—the staggering beauty of the prairie and its life, which we were to experience over and over as we hiked the trails of Wind Cave National Park.

Wind Cave dates back 320 million years, making it one of the world's oldest caverns. The cave system contains fascinating and rare formations as well. Inside the cave, viewers are presented with sights of rare beauty. Wind Cave has one of the largest displays of "boxwork"—a fragile lattice formation made of calcite, which adorns the cave walls and ceilings. Other rare formations contained in the cave include "cave popcorn," "frostwork," and "helictite bushes," whose names are suggestive of their looks. The cave contains few stalactites and stalagmites.

Paha Sapa limestone provides the basis for these formations formed by the action of water deposited on soft rock over millions of years. The waters that seeped into the cave did not flow through but sat stagnant, aiding in the dissolving of Wind Cave's limestone into many passageways. Ancient tepee rings near the cave testify that Native Americans knew a cave existed here, though anthropologists believe the area's earliest peoples refrained from explorations, believing that spirits lurked underground.

The first white settlers to explore the cave were the brothers Jesse and Tom Bingham, who in 1881 heard a strange whistling sound emanating from the earth. The sounds drew them to the hole, which they entered. They soon began offering cavern tours. Explorers then came by the droves and dug many new entrances. On one wall in the Garden of Eden section of

WIND CAVE NATIONAL PARK

the cave eight explorers left their signatures adjacent to the date "8-17-1892." The writing remains as part of the cave's history. In the 100 years since the cave's discovery, spelunkers have explored and mapped 78 miles (125 km) of the cave's complex system. Managers estimate that the figure represents only 5 percent of the total cave, and that literally hundreds of miles remain uncharted. Today we realize that changes in barometric pressure affect the intake or outflow of air from the cave. The flow creates the steady whistling noises that attracted the Binghams.

Recognizing the cave's extraordinary features—as well as the extraordinarily beautiful prairie ecosystem above it—Congress sought protection of the Wind Cave complex, and in 1903 Wind Cave became our seventh national park. Since that time, managers have eliminated solo and private cave explorations, primarily for safety reasons but also for protection of the cave. Professional caving groups called "grottos," with park permission and permits, explore and map uncharted sections of the cave. Cavers desiring to explore Wind Cave should contact one of the participating grottos. Otherwise, visitors may take one of the park-provided, year-round fee tours, led by park personnel who are fully trained in caving. Three tours are available, each costing several dollars. In essence, these cave tours are short subterranean hikes, all of which depart from the Wind Cave Visitor Center.

No longer is it necessary to enter the hole used by early Wind Cave explorers, though you can still see the old entrance by following a trail from the Visitor Center. Simply follow the signs. Of the below-ground hikes, two (The Fairgrounds and the Natural Entrance tours) are 0.5 mile long. A third, The Garden of Eden, is 0.25 mile. Hiking times for these tours vary from 45 minutes to 1.5 hours.

More than 70 miles of "underground trails" lead visitors to examples of boxworks and other formations typical of Wind Cave.

WIND CAVE NATIONAL PARK (PERSPECTIVE)

Wind Cave National Park

STALAGMITES & STALACTITES

TO CUSTER STATE PARK

PICNIC AREA

CAVE ENTRANCE
ELEV. 4080

VISITOR CENTER
ELEV. 4095

CURIOS & LUNCHES

ELEV. 3970

ELEV. 3856

ELEVATOR BUILDING

ASSEMBLY ROOM
(LOWER LANDING)
ELEV. 3865

Source: WCNP

125

Additional special options are offered from June to August, such as the 1-mile Candlelight Tour, during which each visitor carries a candle lantern to illuminate the caverns. Another special event, called the "Caving Tour," involves much crawling over a 3- to 4-hour period. Visitors need reservations and tickets for these tours, available at the visitor center.

After Labor Day the number of tours is reduced to one. Wind Cave offers The Garden of Eden Tour three times a day during the winter months. The Garden of Eden Tour lasts about 1 hour. An elevator plummets 110 feet (the equivalent of eleven stories) into the cave's depths. The water table is located many more feet down at 525 feet, fifty stories deep. Visitors on this tour step from the elevator into a natural, large cavern where tunnels lead off in many directions. The temperature is a constant 53 degrees Fahrenheit throughout the cave, and the humidity varies between 90 and 100 percent. Visitors view the "popcorn" formations as well as the "boxwork," as fragile as it is rare. Hikers learn that cave walls should never be touched, since oils from our skin can damage the formations and stop their growth.

For added fun, the tour leader shuts off the cave electricity—warning visitors in advance. Many people are rendered speechless. An unearthly quiet cloaks the group, and a darkness blacker than any night descends. At last (after maybe 60 seconds) the naturalist strikes a match and lights a lard-pail candle lantern. Everyone gasps. The demonstration suggests how early cave explorers found their way through the dark mazes. The tour is well suited for families. It is fun and informative, offering glimpses of the incredible beauty that is Wind Cave below the ground.

Though better known for its miles of explored underground trails, park visitors can also explore Wind Cave above the ground, in one of the nation's lushest and most pristine prairie grasslands. Here, above the nation's fourth

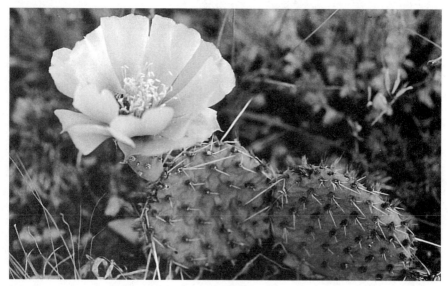

Watch where you sit. Prickly pear is abundant.

longest underground passageway, exists an incredible prairie ecosystem that includes a diverse mix of wildlife roaming freely throughout the park's 28,292 acres (11,450 hectares). Because motorized vehicles and mountain bikes are confined to the park's roads, hikers who venture onto the park's 30 miles (48.3 km) of trails are generally rewarded with unparalleled sightings of wildlife. Hikers see first-hand many of the same grassland conditions that Black Hills pioneers saw in the 1890s.

To keep its environment pristine, Wind Cave has been designated an "indicator park." Researchers here are evaluating the past effects that climate and fire have played on grassland ecology. Look for the small tracts of fenced enclosures intended to exclude bison, elk, deer, and pronghorn antelope. By examining the vegetation inside the fence and comparing it to vegetative growth outside, biologists can monitor the impact of grazing on hardwood species such as aspen, ash, willow, and chokecherry. In this way, scientists hope to better determine the park's carrying capacity for hoofed animals.

Hikers will also see trees, snags, and stumps that have a wedge or cross section cut into them. The marks indicate that biologists have been evaluating the age of the park's trees and forests to determine how often fires burned throughout the area. The information tells biologists how often they should conduct their program of prescribed burning. In the past, fires were an integral part of prairie ecology. Without fires, ponderosa pine would soon replace the lush grasslands hikers now encounter.

Wind Cave National Park offers ten maintained trails, two of which are interpretive trails. Hikers also can combine several trails to make nice, logistically workable loops. With the exception of the Boland Ridge Trail, none of the hikes in this area is very steep; even Boland ascends but a few hundred feet. Several of the longer hikes in Wind Cave National Park require effort simply because the trails wind through the prairie lands for several miles and are at times faint. Once four-wheel-drive roads, these trails can be easily confused with game trails.

If you find yourself lost on one of these routes, hike to a high point and search for landmarks such as a fire tower or nearby road. One ranger/naturalist says that because landmarks are generally visible, Wind Cave National Park provides an excellent setting to refine map-reading skills. Triangulate from the landmark to pinpoint your location and the lost trail. Anticipate confusion by allowing for additional time afield, and remember to carry the following:

1. More water than you think you'll need (and on some summer days it still might not be enough). For a full day's outing in the summer, carry 1 gallon (1.5 liters) per person.
2. Binoculars.
3. Compass and topo map. Trails Illustrated Topo Map No. 238 contains all park trails.
4. Hat and sunscreen.
5. Sturdy boots.
6. Tick spray (in spring and summer).

Much of the park's northwest is designated as a backcountry camping area. No open fires are allowed. If you need a fire to cook, you must carry a backpacker stove. Additionally, hikers must obtain a free backcountry use permit from the visitor center or at the Centennial Trail trailheads; must camp 0.25 mile from any road, out of sight, and 100 feet from any water; and must treat all water. One final suggestion for summer-time prairie hiking: leave early, not only to avoid the heat, but to see the park's wild animals.

Though all trails expose hikers to the prairie ecosystem, each offers fresh perspectives. You simply can't go wrong spending several days hiking all of the Wind Cave above-ground trails. Several people we met had hiked all the trails and now return summer after summer to do so again!

Wind Cave National Park is located in the southeast corner of the Black Hills, an hour's drive south of Rapid City. Take South Dakota Highway 79 south out of Rapid City for 18 miles to Hermosa. From there follow South Dakota Highway 36 to Custer State Park, and take U.S. Highway 16A west through Custer State Park for 10 miles to South Dakota Highway 87. Follow SD 87 south for about 12 miles to the entrance to Wind Cave National Park.

At the junction of SD 87 and U.S. Highway 385, take US 385 south to reach the park's visitor center. You can also access the park by following the "scenic route" of U.S. Highway 85, south from Interstate 90 between Spearfish and Sturgis. Follow US 85 south toward Deadwood, then take US 385 south through the center of the Black Hills until you reach Wind Cave National Park.

Hot Springs is an interesting, friendly little town in the southwest corner of South Dakota, near Wind Cave National Park. Northbound travelers from Nebraska should take US 385 north through Hot Springs and on into the park. Southbound travelers from Rapid City should follow SD 79 south for 48 miles to U.S. Highway 18 west into Hot Springs, then follow US 385 into Wind Cave.

The trails here are all named. They are also designated by number. The park charges no entry fee. Elevation gain is generally so minimal that a description of such is not mentioned in the trail write-ups. Trail profiles are not included in some instances.

General description: A scenic meander through a tallgrass prairie valley that simultaneously explores a canyon in southwest Wind Cave National Park.

Length: 1.4 miles (2.25 km) one-way.

Difficulty: Easy.

Trail maintenance: Good.

Traffic: Light.

Maps: Trails Illustrated topo map No. 238; free Park Service map and brochure of Wind Cave National Park, available at the visitor center.

Finding the trailhead: The trail begins 1.5 miles south of the visitor center on U.S. Highway 385, on the right-hand side of the road.

The hike: The trail begins along an old road that gently descends into a tallgrass prairie valley flanked on one side by a small ridge of ponderosa. The well-marked trail is often frequented by bison—sometimes, in summer, by lone males in rut. Be alert.

The trail proceeds west; shortly the canyon narrows and is further compressed by rock formations that play host to a variety of avian species, including prairie falcons. The trail concludes at a sturdy fence and helps mark the park's western boundary.

The ease of the hike and the abundance and variety of prairie grasses and birdlife combine to make this trail particularly appropriate for family outings.

40   WIND CAVE CANYON TRAIL

General description:	A walk through Wind Cave Canyon, ending at the park boundary fence on the eastern side.
Length:	1.8 miles (2.89 km) one-way.
Difficulty:	Easy.
Trail maintenance:	Good.
Traffic:	Light.
Maps:	Trails Illustrated topo map No. 238; free Park Service map and brochure of Wind Cave National Park, available at the visitor center.

> **See Map on Page 129**

Finding the trailhead: This trail is located on the east side of U.S. Highway 385, 1 mile north of the southern entrance to the park's visitor center. Trail 2 is also an access trail for two other trails, namely, East Bison Flats and the Highland Creek Trail.

The hike: Wind Cave National Park naturalists say this trail is an exceptionally good one for birding, since the abundant limestone cliffs provide nesting grounds for several species, including the great horned owl.

41   EAST BISON FLATS TRAIL

General description:	A prairie hike where wildlife is at times abundant.
Length:	3 miles (4.8 km) one-way.
Difficulty:	Moderately strenuous.
Trail maintenance:	Yearly.
Traffic:	Light.
Maps:	Trails Illustrated topo map No. 238; free Park Service map and brochure of Wind Cave National Park, available at the visitor center.

> **See Map on Page 129**

Finding the trailhead: Depending on the direction from which you plan to hike, the trailhead is located either opposite the visitor center on U.S. Highway 385 (take Wind Cave Canyon Trail Trailhead 2) or 3 miles south of the visitor center on US 385, at Gobbler Pass (Trailhead 3).

The hike: This trail is mildly strenuous, though well marked. From the northern end the trail proceeds southeast along Wind Cave Canyon Trail No. 2 for 0.75 mile. It follows an old road that winds through the canyon offering a cool respite from the summer's prairie heat. Trail No. 2 then intersects with No. 3. Take No. 3, which climbs a short distance to the ridge then proceeds south. Here hikers are offered views north to Rankin Fire Tower.

Bleached buffalo bones in Wind Cave National Park.

Buffalo wallows are numerous in Wind Cave National Park. Sweeping cloud formations characterize the summer sky.

Trail markers have been abundant to this point, but as you proceed through the grasslands some are obscured by tall grasses or have been knocked down by bison. Appropriately, the park has named the prairie through which the trail proceeds Bison Flats. Bison wallows are numerous, and bones picked over by coyotes often litter the ground. Prairie dogs are also abundant. They keep the grass clipped short and stimulate new growth, much preferred by bison. Walk quietly and chances are good that you will see a fat coyote or herd of pronghorn antelope. Stay very alert for bison.

About 0.75 mile after entering the grassland community, the trail ascends a small ridge. Keep left of the ponderosa forest. The boundary fence is to the east and often visible. The trail soon descends to a creek, then cuts sharply west. For the final 0.75 mile, parallel the fence and the road until you reach the southern trailhead, located at the end of the fence on US 385 at Gobbler Pass. From here, you'll need to hitch a ride or meet a previously arranged shuttle back to your vehicle.

42 LOOKOUT POINT–BEAVER CREEK LOOP

General description:	A loop hike that offers a chance to examine both prairie and riparian habitats.
Length:	4 miles (6.43 km).
Difficulty:	Easy to moderately strenuous.
Trail maintenance:	Yearly.
Traffic:	Light.
Maps:	Trails Illustrated topo map No. 238; free Park Service map and brochure of Wind Cave National Park, available at the visitor center.

See Map on Page 129

Finding the trailhead: To access the trailhead from the visitor center, drive north for 1.75 miles on U.S. Highway 385 until it intersects with South Dakota Highway 87. Proceed another 0.5 mile on SD 87, looking closely for logs on the right side of the road indicating the trailhead. If you miss the trail because of high grass, 0.2 mile farther along the road is the Centennial Trail trailhead, which is marked distinctly.

0.0	Trailhead.
1.0	Lookout Point.
1.9	Lookout Point/Highland Creek Trail junction. Go northeast (left).
2.3	Junction with Centennial Trail. Travel west (to the left).
4.0	End of trail, Centennial Trailhead.

Hiking Wind Cave National Park provides rare opportunities for solitude and glimpses of our vanishing American prairie.

The hike: Few trails in the Black Hills offer the opportunity to view both a pristine prairie and riparian ecosystem. The trail is easy with only a few ascents and descents, but some hikers may at times categorize the trail as moderate because of the eight stream crossings, five of which must sometimes be made without the help of logs. Park rangers have placed flattened logs over several of the streams to facilitate crossings. If you do not wish to embark on the entire loop trip, turn back at the end of the Lookout Point Trail, which is 1.9 miles (3.05 km) one-way.

The trail begins by gently rising into a tallgrass prairie ecosystem, characterized by a variety of grasses. In summer, the prairie may show a beautiful progression of wildflowers. After 1 mile of easy walking the trail reaches its highest point at Lookout Point, elevation 4,480 feet. The trail does not lead directly to Lookout Point, but that is just a short jaunt to your right.

From here the trail gently descends and cuts through the northern end of Prairie Dog Canyon. Abundant evidence demonstrates just how these small rodents, acting in concert, can drastically alter the prairie to meet their own requirements. Because prairie dogs must rely for survival on defensive strategies, they have cut the grass to improve their vistas. The changes attract other wildlife species such as bison, coyotes, and rattlesnakes. Be forewarned! One park naturalist who frequently hikes Wind Cave trails says that he must invariably modify his route to avoid a dangerously close approach with bison.

At a trail juncture with the Highland Creek Trail 0.9 mile later, turn left or backtrack on the Lookout Point Trail. If you elect to complete the loop, 2.1 miles (3.4 km) of walking remain. From the junction the trail descends 200 feet to Beaver Creek. As it does, the vegetation changes abruptly to ponderosa pine, the invader. If not checked, ponderosa would soon encroach beyond its historic boundaries and take over much of the prairie here. Prescribed burning curtails its growth.

From Beaver Creek proceed west. About 0.2 mile later, just before it joins the Centennial Trail (see Hike 54), the trail crosses the creek and then does so again four more times. Dry-footed crossings may require imagination and enterprise, particularly following heavy rains.

The hike along Beaver Creek offers views of variegated rock bluffs, some a brilliant orange. High caves cut into the bluffs, and trees that have somehow established a toehold stand as sentinels at the entrances to some of these high rock cuts. Along the stream proper, bootprints of hikers mingle with those of bison and deer, and it is not uncommon to see either.

As the trail nears its end, waters from Cold Spring Creek merge with those of Beaver Creek, which continues its eastern trend. Near the terminus, the trail ascends and shortly concludes at the Centennial Trailhead. Hikers who left their vehicles at the unmarked Lookout Point Trailhead have 0.2 mile to walk south along SD 87 to their vehicles.

43 SANCTUARY–CENTENNIAL–
HIGHLAND CREEK TRAIL

General description:	A one-way route linking several trails in Wind Cave National Park, allowing hikers to experience a variety of park habitats.
Length:	9 miles (14.4 km) one-way. Hikers should arrange for a shuttle ride back to their starting point.
Difficulty:	Moderately strenuous.
Trail maintenance:	Yearly.
Traffic:	Light.
Maps:	Trails Illustrated topo map No. 238; free Park Service map and brochure of Wind Cave National Park, available at the visitor center.

See Map on Page 129

Finding the trailhead: Take U.S. Highway 385 north from the visitor center for 1.5 miles, then take South Dakota Highway 87 north for about 5 miles to the Sanctuary trailhead on the right.

0.0	Sanctuary Trailhead.
0.75	Ascend small saddle.
1.5	Junction with Centennial Trail—take this south.
4.0	Take Centennial Trail to east for 0.5 mile.
4.5	Junction with Highland Creek Trail. Follow this to the right (south).
8.0	Junction with Wind Cave Canyon Trail. Follow this to the right (northwest).
8.5	East Bison Flats Trail comes in from the south. Do not take it.
9.0	End of Wind Cave Canyon Trail. Visitor center is across road.

The hike: The Sanctuary Trail begins its northern terminus where two ecosystems meet: the prairie grassland and the ponderosa pine forest. So much of the suggested 9-mile route weaves in and out of such "edge" conditions that the possibilities of seeing wildlife are excellent. Start early to enhance your chances and, more importantly, to avoid the summer heat.

Within 0.75 of a mile (1.2 km) after departing, the trail ascends slightly and passes over a small saddle. The trail then descends and enters a grassland community in a narrow valley. Periodically, hikers see Lookout Tower on Rankin Ridge. From here the trail cuts up to avoid the wet bottom and continues, though at times indistinctly, to its junction with the Centennial Trail.

Just prior to the link, the Sanctuary Trail passes by what appears to be the remains of an old homestead. All that remains is a rock foundation measuring about 16 by 20 feet and another much smaller rock formation that perhaps formed an old root cellar. Nearby is a small stream.

The prairie here contains a rich assortment of flora and fauna, and it is appropriate that this area can be approached from several different routes and by several different trails. About 2 miles from the trailhead the Centennial and Sanctuary trails cross, and it is at this point that hikers should follow the Centennial Trail, which is easier and more consistently marked.

The Centennial Trail portion of this route proceeds through a series of small rises, passing through a ponderosa forest spotted with pockets of grassland. Bison wallows are numerous. The route approaches its first steep descent 3.5 miles from the Sanctuary Trailhead, and it is here that the hike might be categorized as mildly strenuous, primarily because of the slope. The trail descends from 4,200 feet to 4,020 feet, at which point hikers confront Beaver Creek and a milepost marker.

Leave the Centennial Trail (going right at the fork) and follow a short unnamed trail for 0.25 mile until it intersects with Trail No. 7, the Highland Creek Trail. In times of high water, the trail crosses a "very wet" Beaver Creek three times before it intersects with the Highland Creek Trail. The Highland Creek Trail, which begins 4 miles to the north along Park Road 5, climbs in a southwestern direction almost as quickly as the Centennial Trail dropped. The trail forms a junction with the Lookout Point Trail 0.5 mile later.

Continue following the Highland Creek Trail as it progresses south, then southeast, then south once again through another grassland community. Because you can frequently see the road there is little danger of getting lost. Nevertheless, you may have difficulty remaining on the Highland Creek Trail since it is interlaced with bison trails, which are often more distinct (and hence confusing) than the park trail. If you lose the trail, search for markers by using your binoculars and sweeping right or left. Don't dismay—markers do exist, unless they have been knocked down by bison, which use the markers for scratching posts and in their agony (or ecstacy) sometimes uproot the posts. Because of heavy bison activity in the area, 1.5 miles south of the point where the Highland Trail passes the Lookout Point Trail, some markers may lean and dip into the prairie grass.

About 2.5 miles from the intersection of the Centennial and the Lookout Point trails, the path reenters a thin stand of ponderosa pine then drops 300 feet (from 4,200 feet to 3,900 feet) where, at 2.8 miles after the junction, it intersects with the Wind Cave Canyon Trail. This latter trail is flanked by canyon walls containing a variety of bird nests.

The East Bison Flats Trail junction is reached 0.5 mile later. Continue on the Wind Cave Canyon Trail for 0.5 mile, passing near the park's sewage treatment center to the trail's end across from the visitor center on US 385. You'll have to find a ride to get back to your staring point. Rides from fellow campers seem easy to obtain. Another suggestion, however, is to shuttle vehicles before departing rather than having someone wait at trail's end.

General description:	A loop hike that combines two trails through beautiful grasslands and forests.
Length:	7 miles (11.2 km).
Difficulty:	Easy to moderate.
Trail maintenance:	Yearly.
Traffic:	Light.
Elevation gain:	Minimal.
Maps:	Trails Illustrated topo map No. 238.

See Map on Page 129

Finding the trailhead: Take U.S. Highway 385 north from the Wind Cave National Park visitor center for 0.5 mile, then follow South Dakota Highway 87 north for 7 miles to a "NPS 5" road sign on the right. The Centennial Trail trailhead is 1.25 miles in on the right. The Highland Creek trailhead is 1 mile farther, also on the right.

We suggest leaving your vehicle at the Highland Creek parking lot and beginning the loop hike there. The trail concludes at the Centennial Trailhead, from where you must walk an additional 1 mile back to the vehicle.

0.0	Highland Creek Trailhead, going south.
0.75	Prairie dog town, be alert for snakes.
1.0	Trail marker on top of hill.
3.0	Junction with Sanctuary Trail No. 5. Follow this northwest, to the right.
4.5	Junction with Centennial Trail. Follow this to the northeast (to right).
6.0	Centennial Trail Trailhead and dirt road reached.
7.0	End of 1-mile wald to the east (to vehicle) and the Highland Creek Trailhead.

The hike: This loop option is a relatively flat, natural-history trail, meandering through the high-grass prairie. Throughout, the trail offers scenic vistas of the Black Hills. The final miles pass over a forest trail.

The hike begins on a tallgrass prairie plateau that offers panoramic views. As the trail proceeds, it parallels Rankin Ridge and is separated by about a mile from the Red Valley to the east. In places the trail is faint and markers sometimes infrequent. Be sure your travels proceed in a southeasterly direction. Sharp-tailed grouse are abundant in the high grasslands, and more than one hiker has been unnerved by the flurry of wings that suddenly erupts as feet and bird almost collide.

As the trail descends 0.75 mile from the trailhead, you will find yourself suddenly in the midst of a huge prairie dog town where incessant chirping fills the air. Often the chirps serve not to warn of hikers, but rather of a fat coyote or two lurking near the town's edge. To facilitate defensive vision, prairie dogs have chopped down the grasses. Their efforts help to delineate trail markers, obscured elsewhere by grass. Note also the huge ant mounds throughout.

Upon leaving the prairie dog town, the trail may again be indistinct. Refer to your topo map and compass and notice that the trail now veers slightly southwest (to your right) and parallels a small stand of ponderosa pine. The next trail marker is 0.25 mile away on top of a hill. Stay straight at this point, keeping the pines on your left. As you ascend the next plateau, Rankin Ridge Fire Tower is straight in front of you (2 to 2.5 miles away) and is clearly visible.

The route now heads south. Although game trails might entice you toward the woods, remain on the small ridge. Trail markers will soon lead you south to this trail's intersection with the Sanctuary Trail No. 5 and the Centennial Trail No. 6. Take these trails to the right then remain on No. 5, which proceeds northwest for about 1 mile until it intersects with the Centennial Trail No. 6. Bison wallows and muddy water holes are numerous, as are bison. Here hikers enter a beautiful broad valley. Take time to sit quietly and observe another prairie dog town that, like the others, is often frequented by bison, antelope, deer, and coyotes.

Finally the trail drops to the valley floor where it intersects with the Centennial Trail. Follow this to the right, in a northeasterly direction, where it enters a forest. The remaining 1.25 miles are well marked. About 0.25 mile from the terminus, look for a prescribed burn. At trail's end, someone still has to walk a mile to retrieve the vehicle.

45   BOLAND RIDGE TRAIL

General description:	A one-way trek over Boland Ridge, terminating at the Park boundary fence.
Length:	2.7 miles (4.35 km).
Difficulty:	Moderately strenuous.
Trail maintenance:	Yearly.
Traffic:	Light.
Elevation gain:	Minimal.
Maps:	Trails Illustrated topo map No. 238; free Park Service map and brochure of Wind Cave National Park, available at the visitor center.

> ### See Map on Page 129

Finding the trailhead: Take U.S. Highway 385 north from the Wind Cave National Park visitor center for 0.5 mile, then follow South Dakota Highway 87 north for 7 miles to the "NPS 5" road sign on the right. Proceed on Park Road 5 for 6.4 miles, taking the first dirt road on the left. Go 0.8 mile to the trailhead, on the right.

The hike: The trail mostly traverses gullies and the ridges of Boland Ridge in the Red Valley. Wonderful vistas are offered throughout the valley, the prairies, and, on clear days, of Badlands National Park.

This moderately strenuous hike begins by following a faint dirt road in the high grass prairie. In 0.1 mile hikers cross a tiny creek, which might be dry in times of drought. On our late July hike, the creek was narrow but flowing freely. Whether or not the creek is present depends on capricious weather patterns.

After crossing a meadow, ascend the first ridge of Boland, still on the old, unused road. The trail is well marked, but the markers are only 2 feet high and are often difficult to see in the high grass. The trail follows an easterly and slightly northeast direction and soon encounters another meadow, alive in summer with vibrant wildflowers. Continue along a series of rolling ups and downs as the trail bisects Boland Ridge. Each ascent offers a different perspective. After the last major descent and about 0.5 mile more of hiking, the trail terminates at the park's boundary fence. Now you must retrace your steps.

This area is prime bison habitat (as we discovered that day) and the many gullies easily hide the huge beasts. At times they seem to appear out of nowhere like huge dark shadows. On the day we were there, the majority of the Wind Cave herd had migrated to this area and was in the midst of the age-old annual mating cycle. The noise alone was alarming and could be heard a mile away, sometimes carrying a sound reminiscent of a lion's unthrottled roar. We felt as though we were among the chosen few, watching the herd's behavior for more than an hour. An unexpected prairie hailstorm broke our observation and sent us scurrying for shelter. It also stampeded the herd.

Many trails such as this one in Wind Cave are easily bushwhacked. From Trail 8, roads are visible from the ridges and one could hike along the top of Boland Ridge. As always, carry water, a topo map, and a compass to enhance hiking pleasure, comfort, and safety.

46 RANKIN RIDGE INTERPRETIVE TRAIL

General description: A short interpretive loop trail that ascends through ponderosa pine, providing vistas of Wind Cave National Park and its immense surroundings.

Length: 1 mile (1.6 km).

Difficulty: Moderate.

Trail maintenance: Good.

Traffic: Moderate.

Elevation gain: Minimal.

Maps: An interpretive brochure is available at the park's visitor center.

> *See Map on Page 129*

Finding the trailhead: Take U.S. Highway 385 north from the park's visitor center to South Dakota Highway 87. Take SD 87 north for about 4 miles to the sign and the road for the fire tower, which is on the right. The Rankin Ridge Trailhead is located in the parking lot of the fire tower.

The hike: This short trail provides a delightful climb up Rankin Ridge to sweeping views of the park and beyond. From the ridge the view suggests immense geological phenomena to the east. Red Valley cuts a spectacular swath through the foreground, while the Hog Back Ridge, with Bison Gap, suggests a ring engulfing the Black Hills. The White River Badlands, once a part of the Black hills, shimmer in the distance. The trail is well interpreted and the park provides a booklet (available at the trailhead and visitor center) for the fourteen interpreted stops.

Following the park's suggested route, the trail begins on a northerly aspect. The trail ascends quickly, entering an area that is a prime example of prescribed burning of ponderosa pines. Along the way, several log benches provide opportunities to rest and further explore the panorama sweeping before you. Bring binoculars.

Approximately 0.5 mile from the trailhead, hikers reach the fire tower, elevation 5,013 feet. Seventy-two steps climb to the tower's observation deck. Depending on fire conditions, in summer months the lookout may be staffed. Look west toward the heart of the Black Hills; the ancient updoming effect is apparent. A 0.5-mile descent on a dirt road passes through a ponderosa pine forest and returns you to the parking lot.

General description:	A fun, informative loop hike suitable for the entire family.
Length:	0.75 mile (1.2 km).
Difficulty:	Easy.
Trail maintenance:	Good.
Traffic:	Moderate.
Elevation gain:	Minimal.
Maps:	An interpretive booklet is available at the trailhead or from the park visitor center.

See Map on Page 129

Finding the trailhead: The trail is readily accessible. It is located at Elk Mountain Campground (the only designated campground in Wind Cave National Park), which is about 1.25 miles northwest from the park's visitor center on U.S. Highway 385. The trailhead is opposite the campground's outdoor amphitheater.

The hike: The path winds slightly upwards through a prairie environment. It then enters the woods of Elk Mountain, where the aftermath of a 1991 wildfire is still evident. The interpretive booklet greatly enhances the walk.

BADLANDS NATIONAL PARK

OVERVIEW

The Lakota people call the Badlands Mako Sica, which means "land that is bad." The French trappers who traveled the region in the early 1800s arrived at a similar designation, calling them the *mauvaises terres a traverser*, or "bad lands to travel across." Badlands geology begins with the encroachment of oceans millions of years ago. Over the eons, these waters deposited a multitude of sediments. There followed a series of volcanic activities that contributed to the updoming of the Black Hills and, of course, the uplifting of these sedimentary deposits.

With the updoming, rivers and streams began to flow from the evolving mountains, carrying with them some of the sediments deposited by ancient seas. Eventually these sandstones, banded clays, and limestones were redeposited in what eventually came to be known as the White River Badlands, named for one of the rivers that transported a portion of these materials. Erosional forces then acted on these malleable sediments, creating some of the nation's most spectacular formations.

Today the landscape assumes a multitude of forms, all of which are related to the hardness of the sedimentary deposits and to the manner in which wind and rain, snow and ice chance to act on them. Only the most hardened sandstones remain, assuming a variety of shapes. Some appear as great castles and pyramids, others as fluted spires and mushroom-shaped rocks. When explorers, scientists, visitors, and hikers walked the land they found these bizarre shapes fantastic, as time added more dimension.

Here, too, were the fossilized remains of three-toed horses, prehistoric rhinos and pigs, saber-toothed cats, and an abundance of sea life. Today the 244,300 acres (98,868 hectares) of the White River Badlands serve as a hiker's paradise, since the formations, with their spires and gullies, invite exploration. The Park Service maintains eight short trails in the badlands. In addition, adventurous souls have the opportunity to hike in the nation's largest protected, mixed-grass prairie. What's more, Badlands National Park offers several wilderness areas, which are discussed later in this section.

The shorter, marked trails in Badlands National Park offer hikers opportunities to experience most of the park's geological oddities. With the exception of the Saddle Pass Trail, these are relatively easy and have no significant elevation gain. Combined, these trails require several hours of hiking time, and opportunities abound to study nature and conduct photographic explorations. The Badlands Natural History Association has compiled interpretive booklets for three of the maintained trails: the Fossil Exhibit Trail, the Cliff Shelf Nature Trail, and the Door Trail. Purchase of these inexpensive guides is recommended for those who want to enhance their understanding of badlands topography. None of these trails ascend—or descend—more than a few hundred feet, so trail profiles and details on elevations are not included in this section.

When hiking, please remember the badlands terrain is very fragile. Exercise caution and try to minimize damage by remaining on established paths. Maintain a wary eye for bison and snakes. And carry water, particularly in summer when hiking the longer trails. The Badlands contain no potable water; all must be carried in. Because summer temperatures can and often do exceed 100 degrees, each person needs to carry about a gallon per day. For those contemplating extended trips, packing enough water presents the major obstacle. Open fires are not allowed anywhere in the park so carry a backpack stove. The park does not issue backcountry permits; nevertheless, hikers are advised to stop at the Ben Reifel Visitor Center for weather and wildlife information. Purchase a topo map and discuss trip plans with a ranger. Though park personnel do not mandate registration for wilderness hiking, they do recommend that hikers log their intentions.

Badlands National Park has an open policy for hikers, meaning that there are no closed areas with the exception of black-footed ferret reintroduction sites. Mountain bikes and motorized vehicles are off-limits on all of the park's trails as well as throughout the various wilderness areas. Expect high winds and brief, but violent, thunderstorms year-round.

Badlands National Park is located in the southwestern part of South Dakota, about 70 miles east of the Black Hills of South Dakota. The Ben Reifel Visitor Center is located 83 miles east of Rapid City off Interstate 90 (Exit 109) via the South Dakota State Highway 240 Loop road from Wall, or 72 miles east of Rapid City via South Dakota Highway 44.

Bison skull placed along a Badlands trail to symbolize the buffalo culture, which the government attempted to eradicate. Indian leader Bigfoot rode these rough arid trails just prior to his rendezvous with fate in December of 1890 at nearby Wounded Knee.

Another option is to continue past Wall on I-90 to Exit 131 (Cactus Flat). From there, take South Dakota Highway 240 south for 8.5 miles to the visitor center. For those coming from the south, the other visitor center, White River (open only in summer) is on BIA Highway 27 about 8 miles north of Sharps Corner.

48 CASTLE TRAIL

General description:	A prairie hike flanking the beautiful formations along the Badlands Wall.
Length:	5 miles (8.05 km) one-way.
Difficulty:	Easy.
Trail maintenance:	Good.
Traffic:	Light to moderate.
Maps:	Trails Illustrated Topo Map No. 239, 1:55,000 scale; Department of the Interior Geological Survey topographic map (metric) 43101-F8-PM-050; a free official map and guide pamphlet and interpretive booklets are available at the visitor centers.

Finding the trailhead: Take South Dakota Highway 240 Loop Road northeast from the Ben Reifel Visitor Center for approximately 2 miles to the trail's parking area on the right. The eastern end of the Castle Trail Trailhead is located across the road from the Door, Window, and Notch trails. Access to portions of the trail is also available from the top of the Saddle Pass Trail,

Along the Castle Trail.

145

• CASTLE TRAIL • MEDICINE ROOT LOOP •
• CLIFF SHELF NATURE TRAIL •
• SADDLE PASS TRAIL • FOSSIL EXHIBIT TRAIL •
• THE DOOR, WINDOW, AND NOTCH TRAILS •

about 1.5 miles northwest of the Ben Reifel Visitor Center along the Loop Road. The western terminus of the trail is 5 miles west of the visitor center on SD 240, across the road from the Fossil Exhibit Trail.

0.0   Castle Trail Trailhead.
1.0   Old Northeast Road.
5.0   Fossil Exhibit Trail.

The hike: From the Door and Window trail access, the Castle Trail begins at an elevation of 2,664 feet and progresses through a native mixed-grass prairie while flanking a badlands formations known as the Wall. Castle Trail is the longest of the park's marked trails. After 1 mile, the trail crosses the Old Northeast Road and continues its generally westward course, passing through an assortment of formations that provide mute testimony that the trail deserves the name ascribed to it by the National Park Service. The trail ends across the road from the Fossil Exhibit Trail, 5 miles west of the visitor center, though there is another possibility. Hikers can make a 4-mile loop by hiking west on the Castle Trail for 1 mile then taking the Medicine Root Loop trail west, accessed from the Old Northeast Road. The main trail continues for about 1 mile then loops back east on the Castle Trail for another 2 miles, at which point it returns you to your vehicle. This same type of combination is possible from the west end of the trail.

49   MEDICINE ROOT LOOP

General description: A short hike that offers a connecting loop with the Castle Trail.
Length: 1.5 miles (2.4 km).
Difficulty: Easy.
Trail maintenance: Good.
Traffic: Light to moderate.
Maps: Trails Illustrated topographic map No. 239, 1:55,000 scale; Department of the Interior Geological Survey topographic map (metric) 43101-F8-PM-050; free official map and guide pamphlet and interpretive booklets are available at the visitor centers.

Finding the trailhead: Take South Dakota Highway 240 Loop Road northeast from the Ben Reifel Visitor Center for approximately 2 miles to the trail's parking area on the right. The trailhead is located across the road from the Door, Window, and Notch trails.

Medicine Root Loop can be accessed from either end of the Castle Trail, or from the Saddle Pass Trail, which is 2 miles west of the Ben Reifel Visitor Center.

The hike: The Medicine Root Loop Trail is a flat, easy walk along a narrow dirt path through the grassland area just north of the Castle Trail. As one walks along this plateau, grasslands sweep to the north while the jagged Wall formations rise to the south. Other formations range from short, flat, sod-covered "tables" to lofty spires. The area surrounding the trail is covered with cactus. Grasses hide desert wildflowers. Metal posts are abundant and serve to distinguish the trail from game paths. Medicine Root derives its name from the numerous plants here that were once used by Native Americans. Photo opportunities abound throughout. Medicine Root ends at the junction of Saddle Pass and Castle Trail.

To complete the loop, take the Castle Trail (marked by signs) leading east. From this point the trail ambles along the base of the rock formations. The level trail is somewhat rocky but soon becomes a narrow dirt path.

50   CLIFF SHELF NATURE TRAIL

General description:	An interpretive trail along an ancient cliff shelf that collapsed long ago from the imposing cliffs above.
Length:	0.5 mile (0.8 km).
Difficulty:	Easy.
Trail maintenance:	Good.
Traffic:	Moderate to heavy.
Maps:	Trail booklets may be purchased at the Ben Reifel Visitor Center or at the trailhead box.

See Map on Page 146

Finding the trailhead: The Cliff Shelf Nature Trail can be accessed from a point 0.5 mile east of the Ben Reifel Visitor Center on the Park Loop Road (South Dakota 240).

The hike: Fascinating natural history stories exist here at the collapsed Cliff Shelf, which fell years ago due to underground moisture. The facts of the area are thoroughly interpreted in materials created by the Badlands Natural History Association.

The trail undulates up and down but is wide and has a stairway. A portion of the trail is barrier free and thus wheelchair accessible. The park has provided a rest bench midway through the walk.

51 SADDLE PASS TRAIL

General description:	A short and steep trail through a pass, following a path once used by early travelers.
Length:	Barely 0.5 mile.
Difficulty:	Moderately strenuous.
Trail maintenance:	Yearly.
Traffic:	Light to moderate.
Maps:	Trails Illustrated Topo Map No. 239, 1:55,000 scale; Department of the Interior Geological Survey topographic map (metric) 43101-F8-PM-050; free official map and guide pamphlet and interpretive booklets are available at the visitor centers.

See Map on Page 146

Finding the trailhead: The Saddle Pass Trail can be accessed from the Park Loop Road (South Dakota 240), about 2 miles west of the Ben Reifel Visitor Center.

The hike: The trail begins with an upward scramble through rocks. Simultaneously the trail provides grand vistas of the park, particularly at the summit. At times, especially when wet, the trail can be treacherous—the clay soil turns to "gumbo," which is very slippery and sticky. The trail's dry, loose stones can sometimes act like ball bearings.

At the summit, the Saddle Pass Trail links with both the Castle Trail and the Medicine Root Loop Trail. From here, hikers have a choice of descending on the route they traveled upward or linking with one of these two trails.

In the early days, travelers from the north proceeding south to the town of Interior would leave their buggies at the top of the trail. They would then attempt to coax horses down the steep track. If the horses balked, riders left them here with the buggies, retrieving them upon their return from Interior.

52 FOSSIL EXHIBIT

General description:	A short, barrier-free loop to an exhibit of area fossils.
Length:	0.25-mile (0.4-km) loop.
Difficulty:	Extremely easy.
Trail maintenance:	Good.
Traffic:	Moderate to heavy.
Maps:	A self-guiding booklet is available at the trail kiosk or visitor center.

See Map on Page 146

Finding the trailhead: The Fossil Exhibit Trail is located 5 miles west of the Ben Reifel Visitor Center on the Park Loop Road (South Dakota 240).

The hike: At the Fossil Exhibit, Badlands National Park has created replicas of fossils indigenous to the Badlands, and they are exhibited along this trail in glass-covered bins.

53 THE DOOR, WINDOW, AND NOTCH TRAILS

See Map on Page 146

General description:	Easy journeys to view some of the park's most rugged rock formations.
Length:	The Door Trail, 0.66 mile (1.06 km) round-trip; the Window Trail is 0.25 mile (0.4 km); the Notch Trail is 1.5 mile (2.4 km) round-trip.
Difficulty:	Easy for Door and Window trails; easy to moderate for Notch Trail.
Trail maintenance:	Good, though the rock and soil here means that trails can sometimes be rough.
Traffic:	Heavy.
Maps:	A self-guiding brochure for these trails is available at the trailhead or visitor center. The numbered posts are small and can be difficult to locate.

Finding the trailhead: The trails are accessible from a parking lot 2 miles east of the Ben Reifel Visitor Center, along Park Loop Road 240.

The hike: The first 100 yards of the **Door Trail** are barrier free and allow handicapped visitors to enter and pass through the "door," to see some of the Badlands' most rugged terrain. The rest of the trail is rough but flat, and sturdy shoes are recommended. Off-trail the terrain is fragile and many edges are loose. Exercise caution!

A Badlands skyline.

Throughout the area hikers are treated to vast panoramas of spires, "doors in the walls," and steep gullies. Because of the interplay of light, the design changes constantly—almost whimsically—creating a photographer's paradise, especially in the morning and early evening. Nothing here is ever the same.

The **Window Trail** is an easy walk to a natural "window" in the Badlands Wall, through which visitors can peek at a stupendous view of the eroded canyon. The trail is also barrier free, though trail conditions can be rough.

The **Notch Trail** is a hike of great beauty, but one not recommended to those with a fear of heights. For the first 0.25 mile, it meanders through the canyon floor around rocks and delicate prairie flowers. Then it reaches a sixty-one-rung ladder, which is cabled into the hill. Here's where those afraid of heights will have to turn back.

Upon reaching the top of the ladder, follow the scuffed trail that winds around rock ledges above the canyon for about 0.5 mile until it emerges and ends at the top of a cliff, providing a commanding overlook of the valley. This is part of a cliff that collapsed long ago and formed the Cliff Shelf Nature Trail, lying directly below.

Approach to the ladder.

ADDITIONAL HIKES

For those interested in exploring the badlands wilderness, the park offers several options that provide liberal access. Badlands National Park encompasses the nation's largest prairie wilderness, which hikers may roam at will. Leave the road behind and explore the Sage Creek Wilderness Area, which extends over 64,144 acres (25,959 hectares), or trek the Stronghold and Palmer Creek units in the Pine Ridge Indian Reservation, though still managed by the Park.

Sage Creek Wilderness Area

From the Ben Reifel Visitor Center, take the Park Loop Road (South Dakota Highway 240) west for 24 miles (38.6 km) to Sage Creek Rim Road, which comes in from the left. Follow this road for 5.9 miles to a turnout on the left. A camper registration box is located here and animal/people trails can be seen wandering into the wilderness area. No marked trails exist in the wilderness areas, but half the fun results from striking out on your own.

Another option is to follow the Sage Creek Rim Rd. for 11 miles (17.7 km) to the Sage Creek Campground (32 miles from the Ben Reifel Visitor Center). Again, there are no designated trails from the campground; however, a multitude of animal/people paths strike out from here. Most of the trails soon give out and hikers are on their own to wander at will in solitude and the land's overwhelming beauty.

More than five hundred bison call Sage Creek home. Use extreme caution around these large mammals, especially during the rut season (July through September). Do not approach within 200 yards.

About one-third of the Sage Creek Wilderness landscape consists of eroded and nearly barren badlands. The remainder of the park consists of a mixed-grass prairie ecosystem. Though hikers may see wildlife in most Badlands areas, the park's remote wilderness tends to attract the largest wildlife concentrations. Look for coyotes, prairie dogs, sharp-tailed grouse, wild turkeys, eagles, rabbits, and hawks as well as for bison, pronghorn, mule deer, and even bighorn sheep.

Stronghold and Palmer Creek Units

The Stronghold and Palmer Creek areas are within the Pine Ridge Reservation in the southwestern part of the Badlands National Park. The White River Visitor Center is located between the two. Potential users should first inquire at the visitor center to determine prevailing conditions, particularly for the more remote Stronghold Unit. Visitors must cross private land for most access; please be very respectful of private property.

To reach this area, proceed southwest from the Ben Reifel Visitor Center for 2.5 miles to the town of Interior. Take South Dakota Highway 44 west for 39 miles to the town of Scenic. From Scenic, follow Forest Roads 589 and 27 south for 20 miles to the White River Visitor Center. Or, from the Wounded Knee site in southwestern South Dakota, take FR 27 north. The White River Visitor Center is 8 miles north of Sharps Corner.

The wilderness areas of Badlands National Park intrigue because of the freedom they offer. Hikers can strike off in any direction. Wander through bluffs and prairie grass, or follow dry streambeds. In these areas, hikers can find solitude, peace, and a stark beauty found nowhere else.

Backpackers venturing into the wilderness are free to roam at will, camping throughout, providing they are at least 0.5 mile off the road and not visible to traffic. Park officials also ask you to remember that others will follow your example, and ask that you help preserve the land by practicing low-impact camping. Do not disturb any fossils or artifacts you might find, but do report any finds to park rangers.

The Lakota people consider the Stronghold area sacred. Please do not touch any cultural artifacts.

THE LONG TRAILS

The Black Hills are great terrain for hikers, and include two longer routes for those who cannot get enough of the country.

54   THE CENTENNIAL TRAIL

OVERVIEW

The Centennial Trail has a lofty beginning and magnificent ending. If one proceeds from north to south, the trail begins at Bear Butte and Bear Butte Lake, where Crazy Horse presided over a Council of Nations that was determined to protect the Black Hills from outside encroachment. The trail ends in Wind Cave National Park, an area best known for its subterranean features but equally touted for its rolling prairie features that host many natural dramas that have their pinnings in grass.

The land between Bear Butte and Wind Cave is equally as inspiring. Here, the curtain goes up daily, for there are lakes, peaks, historic areas, and landscapes that teem with wildlife and provide hikers with endless variety. What all this distills down to is that the Centennial Trail does precisely what it was established to do: it provides users with an opportunity to relive the fabulous history that is South Dakota's, and to evaluate for themselves what magnificent natural treasures the state still retains.

The Centennial Trail can be backpacked in one grand outing or can be hiked segmentally. Mountain bikes are permitted in most areas, except for the nationally designated wilderness area and in National Park Service-administered areas of Wind Cave and Mount Rushmore. For those planning an extended Centennial trek, about the only real concern is potable water. That problem can be solved by carrying a water filter.

Finding campsites is not a problem, since these can be fashioned nearly anywhere in the wilderness and primitive settings. Backpackers are encouraged to make primitive use of the land, using no-trace camping methods. In Custer State Park camping is permitted only in the French Creek Natural Area and in Iron Creek Horse Camp. For all other areas, tenters must camp off the trail and essentially out of sight. As well, hikers must use good camping hygiene.

The Centennial Trail is 111 miles long, and assuming the somewhat moderate pace of about 10 miles each day, the entire trail can be covered in ten to twelve days. Obviously backpackers will need to become students of lightweight food products or toss in the towel and rely on the lightweight foods generally sold out of sporting good stores.

For those preferring to hike segmentally, the Centennial Trail provides twenty-two trailheads, conveniently located for excursions of 4 to 10 miles.

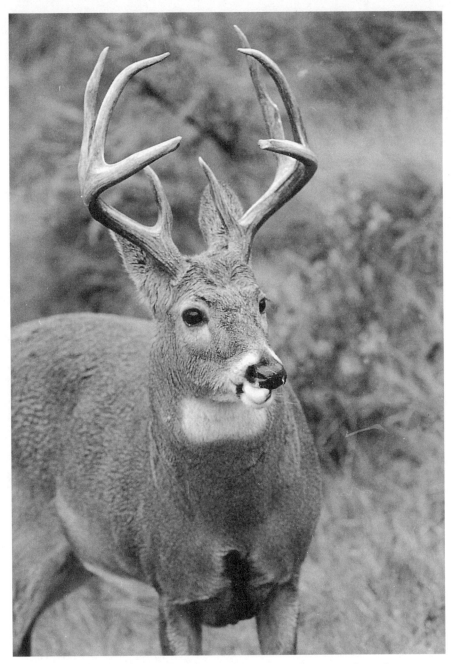

Visitors frequently see deer throughout the 110-mile Centennial Trail.

Campsites often are located near the trailheads or along the route. If, so, we have noted them.

The following provides a breakdown of trailheads and highlights the major features hikers will encounter between each trailhead. For many, hiking the trail segmentally may well satisfy limitations imposed by time constraints. Trail users will be delighted to learn that with but few exceptions, the Centennial Trail is very well marked.

TRAILHEADS (NORTH TO SOUTH)

Bear Butte Campground (Mile 0)

From the crest of Bear Butte, the trail drops 4 miles, passing the Bear Butte Visitor Center and soon crossing South Dakota Highway 79, where it proceeds past Bear Butte Lake. From the lake, the trail courses across grasslands and enters, at mile 6, the Fort Meade Recreation Area. The prairie trail continues for another 2 miles, crossing South Dakota Highway 34 near Fort Meade Veterans Hospital.

For a fee, the state offers a campground on Bear Butte Lake. The campground is conveniently located and provides hikers with a jumping-off point as well as an ideal spot from which to view the myriad waterfowl. Alternately, at about mile 6, a primitive campsite could be fashioned near the crest just before the trail drops down to the more civilized surroundings of the Veterans Administration Center at Fort Meade, which offers no camping.

Fort Meade Trailhead (Mile 10.5)

Follow SD 34 from Sturgis for 2 miles to the historic military post by the same name. From here, this short segment proceeds south and approaches the famous Fort Meade Cemetery.

Alkali Creek Trailhead (Mile 12.5)

From Sturgis follow SD 34 for 5 miles to the trailhead. From here, the trail proceeds south and parallels the general flow of Alkali Creek for about 5 miles, rising steeply as it progresses. The trail then proceeds in an up-and-down manner until its junction with the next trailhead.

Elk Creek Trailhead (Mile 23.5)

From Sturgis, drive south along Forest Road 170 to Forest Road 135, then to Forest Road 168. From here, the trail proceeds along a small creek, which in September is often dry, for almost 2 miles. It then ascends through stands of ponderosa that provide ideal elk habitat. Bands of elk wander here, and

THE CENTENNIAL TRAIL

To 212
Bear Butte State Park
Bear Butte Lake Trailhead
To Spearfish
Fort Meade Recreation Area
79
90
Fort Meade Trailhead
Bear Butte Lake
Bear Butte Creek
Sturgis
34
Alkali Creek
Alkali Creek Trailhead
N
170
0   2.5   5
Miles
Elk Creek Trailhead
Elk Creek
136
234
To Rapid City
Dalton Trailhead
Boxelder Creek Trailhead
Nebo
Pilot Knob Trailhead
Boxelder Creek
Deer Creek Trailhead
Rapid Creek Trailhead
Tamarack Gulch Trailhead
161
Silver City
44
To Rapid City
Pactola Reservoir
385
Brush Creek Trailhead
To Hill City

THE CENTENNIAL TRAIL

alert hikers see them often.

After ascending the ridge, the trail drops precipitously into the Elk Creek drainage, where a sign advises trail users that they must determine whether they wish to proceed along a primitive, unmaintained trail that parallels Elk Creek or follow the maintained horse trail. Whichever trail hikers select eventually routes users to the canyon edge where it ascends very steeply for about 0.5 mile to a logging road. Pay close attention here, for Centennial Trail markers may be limited; a number of logging roads in this area resemble the trail and often create confusion and momentary panic. In one area, where the trail intersects with three logging roads all at the same spot, it can become darn confusing. Take time to search for the markers. If you follow a road for several hundred yards and don't see a Centennial Trail marker, assume you've made a wrong turn. Retrace your steps and look again. Markers do exist, though time may have dimmed them.

This section of the trail is 10.9 miles long, and at mile 33 (8.6 miles from this trailhead), the trail passes through a fence and enters a jeep road, which it follows for slightly more than a mile. The trail then becomes a traditional trail and remains as such until it concludes at Dalton Trailhead.

Possible campsites are numerous, particularly in the Elk Creek drainage. There is also a campsite at Dalton Lake where hikers can replenish their water supply.

Dalton Trailhead (Mile 32.4)

From Sturgis, access Forest Road 170 and follow it 4 miles to its intersection with Forest Road 26. Follow FR 26 for 10 miles until it intersects with Forest Road 224. This section of trail proceeds through dense stands of timber and is alive with populations of deer.

South Boxelder Creek Trailhead (Mile 40.6)

Same as to Dalton, but remain on FR 26 for 3.5 miles until the road intersects with Forest Road 140. Like the preceding section, this one also contains nice populations of deer.

Boxelder Forks Campground–Pilot Knob Trailhead (Mile 46.6)

This section of the Centennial Trail is most easily accessed from Hill City by following U.S. Highway 385 north past Sheridan Lake and Pactola Reservoir. From Pactola, proceed about 8 miles to Forest Road 208. Follow FR 208 for 0.5 mile to the trailhead.

Deer Creek Trailhead (Mile 49.8)

Same as the preceding, except from Pactola Reservoir, proceed only 2 miles to Forest Road 299.

Rapid Creek Trailhead (Mile 54.4)

View from the Centennial Trail near Sheridan Lake.

Proceed north of the Pactola Visitor Center, following US 385 to about the middle of the dam. Take a hard right onto the Pactola Basin Road, which begins on top of the dam. The trailhead is located at the base of the dam.

Tamarack Gulch Trailhead (Mile 54.9)

Same directions as for Rapid Creek Trailhead, but proceed 0.5 mile farther along the Basin Dam Road. Signs point to the respective trailheads.

Brush Creek Trailhead (Mile 59.4)

From US 385 turn east onto Forest Road 159, which you must follow for 2.6 miles down a dirt road to the trailhead. Proceeding south, the trail climbs several hills and descends 5 miles later on Dakota Point, located on Sheridan Lake.

Dakota Point Trailhead (Mile 64.4)

Follow US 385 past Sheridan Lake to the Sheridan Lake Road. Proceed 1 mile to the trailhead.

Spring Creek Trailhead

About the same as the previous trailhead, though Spring Creek provides a 0.2-mile spur access.

Flume Trailhead (Mile 66.1)

This trailhead is located adjacent to the Sheridan Lake Campground. Follow the signs to the South Marina. At 1 mile from this trailhead the trail crisscrosses the Centennial Trail. Hikers then have the option of proceeding farther along the Flume Trail (see Hike 35) or proceeding either north or south along the Centennial Trail proper.

Samelius Trailhead (Mile 71.1)

Located just north of U.S. Highway 16. Hikers from this point will quickly proceed through a tunnel, which passes under US 16. Three miles later the trail links with the Big Pine Trailhead, described in subsequent paragraphs.

Willow Creek Trailhead and Horse Camp

Provides a 4-mile spur to the Centennial Trail, which departs from near the KOA Campground along South Dakota Highway 244.

Big Pine Trailhead (Mile 74.1)

The 8.3-mile stretch between Big Pine and Iron Creek trailheads begins on the north side of SD 244 (about 3 miles east of Mount Rushmore) where it progresses south. Within a mile, the trail passes a spur linking with the Willow Creek Trailhead. From here, the trail ascends steeply, passing Elk Horn Mountain and enters the Black Elk Wilderness Area, periodically offering views of Harney Peak.

About 4 miles from the trailhead this segment of the Centennial Trail passes within a mile of Mount Rushmore. About 5 miles from the trailhead, the trail departs the Black Elk Wilderness and continues its general downward progression to the Iron Creek Trailhead, located in Custer State Park.

In Custer, the trail follows a progression of beaver dams then departs the stream where it assumes an easy up-and-down progression, passing over a series of small hills.

Iron Creek Trailhead (Mile 82.4)

From the Peter Norbeck Visitor Center in Custer State Park, follow US 16A west for 5.2 miles until the road intersects with South Dakota Highway 87N. Follow SD 87 for 5.7 miles to the sign for the trailhead. Follow the dirt road for 0.1 mile to the trailhead sign. The Centennial Trail is located between the sign and exit from the dirt road back to SD 87.

Badger Hole Trailhead (Mile 89.7)

From the Peter Norbeck Visitor Center, take US 16A west for 5.5 miles to the turnoff on the left for the Badger Hole. Proceed 1 mile to the trailhead, which links to the short road to the Charles Badger Clark Memorial (See Hike 22).

This 4.2-mile continuation of the Centennial Trail begins by swinging around a local water-treatment plant. The trail then ascends into a burn area, interesting as it provides a bird's-eye view of plant succession following a fire. The trail progresses over rolling landscape, mixed with ponderosa and prairie grass. Wildlife, including bison, abound.

French Creek Horse Camp Trailhead (Mile 93.9)

See Hike 16 for location of the French Creek trailhead and an elaboration of the trail's features in this area.

Highland Creek Trailhead (Mile 104.2)

This trailhead is accessed most easily from NPS Park Road 5 located in the northern portion of Wind Cave National Park. The road is dirt and must be followed for about 2 miles before reaching this access point.

This 6.2-mile segment departs from a prairie setting and wanders through stands of ponderosa pine (see Hike 44). It provides the possibility of encounters with bison, prairie dogs, elk, and pronghorn antelope. It offers periodic views of Rankin Ridge Lookout and glimpses of a dynamic prairie ecosystem as well.

Norbeck Lake Trailhead (Mile 110.4)

Depending on your route, this trailhead will be either the beginning or the ending of your Centennial Trail hike. Or it might represent the start and finish of a day outing. Either way, you are in for some exciting times.

Access this trailhead from near the Wind Cave Visitor Center. Follow US 385 north for about 1 mile, then take the right turn near the prairie dog town for SD 87, which you must then follow north for 1.5 miles. The trailhead is on your right.

55 GEORGE S. MICKELSON TRAIL

OVERVIEW

According to its namesake and founder, George S. Mickelson, "This trail may be our last opportunity to provide a pathway that is easily used by the elderly, people with disabilities and the very young, as well as hikers, bicyclists and other more traditional trail users." Begun in 1991, the Mickelson Trail represents a dream that is just now unfolding. Currently, only about half of the trail has been completed, but with some luck, all 110 miles should be in place in a few years.

The concept was conceived in part by South Dakota Governor George Mickelson, who intended that a trail should pass through the heart of the Black Hills. Mickelson envisioned a trail that would follow the historic Burlington Northern Railroad from Deadwood to Edgemont, which was abandoned from 1983 to 1989. In response to the abandonment, a group of local citizens decided to preserve the rail line corridor and develop a recreation trail. Mickelson remained a strong advocate of the trail, but was unable to see his vision completed. Following his untimely death in 1993, the trail was named in his honor.

Almost the entire trail has been mapped out, though financial—and sometimes political—constraints have prevented the trail's entire construction. Cooperation between public and private entities and funding from private sources are needed to speed construction. Tax-deductible contributions may be made to the Game, Fish and Park Foundation or to the Friends of the George S. Mickelson Trail. For more information, contact the South Dakota Division of Parks and Recreation, 523 East Capitol Avenue, Pierre, SD 57501-3182, or call (605) 773-3391.

When completed, this trail along an old railbed will offer glimpses into the history of the Black Hills. From it you'll see old gold camps, claim cabins, cliff cuts, hardrock tunnels, high trestles, and pristine streams, as well as more modern creations such as the Crazy Horse Memorial. In many places the old railbed is remote enough to offer a backcountry experience. Already many such opportunities are available, for about 50 miles of the trail have been completed, specifically a 30-mile section between Hill City

The Mickelson Trail approaches the evolving Crazy Horse Memorial.

and Pringle and a 17-mile section between Deadwood and Dumont. Work continues between the towns of Dumont and Hill City.

Non-hiking trail users age sixteen and older are required to pay a $2 per day or a $6 per season user fee. Hikers are not assessed, nor are those using the trail within the city limits of Deadwood, Lead, Rochford, Hill City, Custer, and Pringle. Though we hiked all that was open, we offer here only a generalized description. So much is in a state of change, and the few things we found in need of improvement may well be satisfactory after additional contributions roll in. Check with local authorities, the Forest Service, or the South Dakota Game and Fish Department about trail status, and let them know of your interest.

The segment from Deadwood to Dumont offers six trailheads. If one proceeds north to south as we did, the trail is generally uphill, passing through forests and some private farmland, which the trail skirts.

Deadwood and Kirk Trailheads

The trail leaves the town of Deadwood, then skirts the town of Lead and climbs until it overlooks Lead and the various mining operations of the Homestake Mining Company. After departing Lead, the trail passes through remote areas of timber alternating with farms and meadows. In places the trail is steep, though it levels near the Englewood Trailhead.

Locate the Deadwood Trailhead in Deadwood on Highway 85 at the Deadwood Gulch Lodge, and find the Kirk Trailhead just south of Lead.

GEORGE S. MICKELSON TRAIL

Trailhead
Deadwood
To Sturgis
Lead
85
Kirk Area
Opened 1991
To Cheyenne
Crossing
Dumont
385
Trailhead
17
44
To Rapid City
Rapid
Creek
Castle Creek
Creek
Pactola Lake
17
Deerfield Lake
Sheridan Lake
Spring Creek
Hill City
To Mt. Rushmore
Trailhead
N
Trailhead
0   5   10
Miles
To Custer
State Park
Custer
Custer Parkway
Opened 1992
16
To Newcastle
385
Pringle
To Wind Cave
National Park
89
Trailhead
18
To Hot Springs
Edgemont
To Mule Creek Junction, WY
18

Sugarloaf Trailhead

Access this just 2 miles south of Lead on US 85.

Whitewood Creek, Englewood, and Dumont Trailheads

Follow US 385 for 8 miles south to its junction at Brownsville with FR 227 (just across from Nemo Road). Follow this road west for 5 miles until it intersects with Forest Road 205. Whitewood Creek Trailhead is 3.5 miles north of this intersection; Englewood Trailhead is in 1 mile. Dumont Trailhead is on FR 205 just 3 miles south of its intersection with Forest Road 227.

The other segment of the Mickelson Trail now open passes from Hill City to Custer then goes on to Pringle, where the Mickelson Trail ends. A convenient access point for the trail in Hill City is near the south end of town at the one of the campgrounds. The trail proceeds along a level course for several miles before it climbs and scurries over the pass near the Crazy Horse Memorial.

From here the trail proceeds downhill to the Custer Trailhead, located in the town of Custer. From Custer the trail climbs slightly but generally maintains a level course to its junction with the Pringle Trailhead 14 miles later. This segment of the trail parallels Beaver Creek, which in places is a particularly beautiful waterway.

Other segments of the Mickelson Trail have been completed and are serving hikers using other trails. These are only short segments, however, and they are mentioned in this book's hike descriptions only when they combine to form a route for another system of trails.

The Mickelson Trail is nearing completion but already provides access to the area's mining history as well as to a variety of natural features.

APPENDIX A SUGGESTED EQUIPMENT

Even the most experienced hiker is sometimes well into a hike when he or she remembers a forgotten but necessary item. The following list is intended to help in preventing such occurrences, ensuring a more enjoyable trip. Some items on the list are essentials, but others can be included according to personal preference. Always keep the weight factor in mind—unless you can pack as much as a llama or a horse.

Weather in the Black Hills can be fickle. Thundershowers come on a regular basis in the summer months. And if you're high on a mountain trail during a sudden shower, it can get very cold suddenly. So even if it's 75 degrees at your campsite, carry enough warm clothes and good rain gear to be prepared. Hiking boots should be of good quality and already broken in. Many a trip has been ruined in the first few hours by new or poorly fitting boots. If you've purchased something new for a hike (tent, backpack, boots, etc.), it's a good idea to try it out, break it in, or set it up before embarking on your trek.

One final caution about drinking the water. Don't. Don't drink it until it has been purified with an acceptable system, that is. Wind Cave National Park and Badlands National Park have little water, and both these places are hot and dry in the summer. The advice of most rangers in the Black Hills is to pack your own water. Take the water weight factor into account when planning a hike of any length.

The following checklists will help you pack well for any day or backpack trip in the Black Hills:

Clothing

☐ Good quality raingear
☐ Warm jacket
☐ Windbreaker
☐ Wind pants
☐ Long underwear
☐ Long pants
☐ Lightweight long-sleeve shirt(s)
☐ T-shirts and shorts
☐ Sweater or heavy shirt
☐ Socks for each day plus one set extra
☐ Underwear
☐ Hats, one wool, one with sun visor
☐ Gloves
☐ Belt
☐ Good hiking boots
☐ Extra shoes or sandals for camp and stream crossings

Food:

- ☐ Hot and cold drink mixes (tea, coffee)
- ☐ Dry food (dry your own or buy the commercial kind of meals, rice, beans, noodles)
- ☐ Hot cereal to mix with water
- ☐ Trail mix (make your own)
- ☐ High-energy snacks

Hiking equipment:

- ☐ Tent and rain fly
- ☐ Warm sleeping bag and pad with stuff sacks
- ☐ Full-size backpack
- ☐ Day pack for shorter side trips from a base camp
- ☐ Backpack stove and fuel
- ☐ Cooking pot
- ☐ Cup
- ☐ Bowl
- ☐ Utensils
- ☐ Water bottle
- ☐ Waterproof matches in container

Miscellaneous:

- ☐ Compass
- ☐ Maps
- ☐ Tick and insect repellent
- ☐ Sunscreen and lipscreen
- ☐ Sunglasses
- ☐ Toilet paper
- ☐ Toothbrush
- ☐ Biodegradable soap
- ☐ Small towel/washcloth
- ☐ Small backpack shovel
- ☐ Garbage sack
- ☐ Plastic sandwich bags
- ☐ Pocket knife
- ☐ Binoculars
- ☐ Water filter or purification tablets
- ☐ First-aid kit
- ☐ Flashlight and batteries
- ☐ Camera and film
- ☐ Fishing gear and license
- ☐ Pocket notebook and pencil
- ☐ 50-foot length of nylon cord
- ☐ Waterproof backpack cover
- ☐ Paperback book

APPENDIX B MANAGING AGENCIES

The following agencies are excellent sources for maps, hiking and camping information and reservations, books, and other materials concerning the Black Hills.

USDA FOREST SERVICE

Bearlodge Ranger District
U.S. Highway 14 East, Box 680
Sundance, WY 82729
(307) 283-1361

Elk Mountain Ranger District
1225 Washington Boulevard
Newcastle, WY 82701
(307) 746-2783

Custer Ranger District
330 Mount Rushmore Road
Custer, SD 57730
(605)673-4853

Pactola/Harney Ranger District
23939 Highway 385
Hill City, SD 57745
(605) 574-2534

Nemo Ranger District
U.S. Highway 14A East, Box 407
Deadwood, SD 57732
(605)578-2744

Pactola Ranger District
803 Soo San Drive
Rapid City SD 57702
(605) 343-1567

**Black Hills National Forest
Visitor Center**
U.S. Highway 385 at Pactola Reservoir
(17 miles north of Hill City, SD)
(605) 343-8755

Spearfish Ranger District
2014 North Main
Spearfish, SD 57783
(605) 642-4622

**Black Hills National Forest
Supervisor's Office**
RR 2, Box 200
Custer, SD 57730
(605) 673-2251

OTHER AGENCIES

Bear Butte State Park
Box 688
Sturgis, SD 57785
(605) 347-5240

**Black Hills Parks and Forest
Association**
RR 1, Box 190-WCNP
Hot Springs, SD 57747
(605) 745-4600

Bureau of Land Management
310 Roundup
Belle Fourche, SD 57717
(605) 892-2526

Bureau of Land Management
1225 Washington Boulevard
Newcastle, WY 82701
(307) 746-4453

Custer State Park
HC 83, Box 70
Custer, SD 57730
(605) 255-4515

Devils Tower National Monument
Box 8
Devils Tower, WY 82714
(307) 467-5283

Wind Cave National Park
RR 1, Box 190
Hot Springs, SD 57747
(605) 745-4600

Mount Rushmore National Memorial
Box 268
Keystone, SD 57751
(605) 574-2523

Wyoming Division of Tourism
I-25 at College Drive
Cheyenne WY 82002
(800) 225-5996

South Dakota Department of Tourism
711 E. Wells Avenue
Pierre, SD 57501-3369
(800) 732-5682

APPENDIX C CAMPGROUNDS AND MAPS

CAMPGROUNDS

Campgrounds are abundant in the Black Hills, ranging from those with facilities to ones that are primitive and not so easily accessible. There is something for everyone. Some require reservations, so it's a good idea to call ahead, especially during the busier summer months. For those unable to plan ahead, keep in mind that, as a general rule, the unreserved sites become available early in the morning as others pull out. Campgrounds on or near lakes and those offering shower facilities seem to fill the fastest.

Backcountry or wilderness camping is allowed in most of the Black Hills and Badlands National Park. Some areas require a backcountry camping permit, and all areas have certain regulations, which can be obtained from the visitor centers or ranger stations. Practice no-trace camping wherever you go.

Wind Cave

1 campground, Elk Mountain, located 1 mile from the visitor center. Water and restrooms from spring through fall.

Custer State Park

7 campgrounds with individual sites (and water and showers). Some are reserved, some are first-come sites. Call (800) 710-2267 for reservations. Additionally, there are 2 primitive camping sites in the French Creek Natural Area.

Black Hills National Forest

28 campgrounds; all but 3 have drinking water from spring to fall. To reserve, call (800) 280-2267.

Bearlodge Mountains

3 campgrounds in the vicinity of the Black Hills trails: Cook Lake, Reuter Campground, and Sundance Campground.

Badlands National Park

2 campgrounds. Cedar Pass Campground is located near the Ben Reifel Visitor Center and has water and restrooms. Winter camping is free here. Sage Creek Primitive Campground is in the Sage Creek Wilderness Area, has no water, and campfires are not permitted.

MAPS

Several types of maps are available for the Black Hills hiker and can be obtained at the visitor centers, the agency offices, and at sporting goods stores throughout the area. Maps may also be obtained by writing or calling the agencies. Many are free, others are available for purchase. The free maps, descriptive booklets, and trail guides offered by the Forest Service, Custer State Park, Wind Cave National Park, and Badlands National Park serve as excellent guides.

Providing completely accurate mileages of trails is difficult, and hikers should bear in mind that the trails may be slightly shorter or longer than indicated. Additionally, sometimes the trail lengths differ on the maps from what is posted on the trail signs. More important than the actual length though, is often the difficulty rating. A very strenuous trail of 2 miles often seems and takes longer than an easy one of 5 miles.

The Black Hills National Forest Map, $3, with a scale of 2 miles to the inch, is available at visitor centers and USDA Forest Service offices.

Quad and topographical maps may be obtained for a fee from visitor centers and USDA Forest Service offices, as well as from the following:

Trails Illustrated
P.O. Box 3610
Evergreen, CO 80439
(303) 670-3457
(800) 962-1643

Maps available:
Black Hills South, No. 238
Black Hills Northeast, No. 751
Badlands National Park, SD No. 239.

U.S. Geological Survey National Mapping Division
12201 Sunrise Valley Drive
Mail Stop 809
Reston, VA 22092
(703) 648-7070

Branch of Distribution
USGS Federal Center,
Denver, CO 80225

APPENDIX D SELECTED READING

Many of the following books were helpful resources as we prepared this book. Others make fascinating reading. The Natural History Association of the Black Hills has available a wonderful selection of books for all ages. The visitor centers within the Black Hills also have a great inventory of books for sale. Topics available in both places include natural history, history, Native American history and lore, hiking advice, children's books, and coloring books. The list is extensive.

A Practical Guide to Outdoor Protection: Sawyer Products, 1994.

Dodge, Richard Irving. *The Black Hills*: 1876.

Fletcher, Colin. *The Complete Walker III*. New York: Alfred A. Knopf, 1974.

Froiland, Sven G. *Natural History of the Black Hills and Badlands.* Sioux Falls, So. Dak.: Augustana College Center For Western Studies, 1990.

Harmon, Will. *Wild Country Companion.* Helena, Mont.: Falcon Press Publishing Co., Inc., 1994.

Moeller, Bill and Jan Moeller. *Crazy Horse, His Life, His Lands: A Photographic Biography.* Beautiful America Publishing Co., 1987.

Raventon, Edward. *Island in The Plains, A Black Hills Natural History.* Boulder, Colo.: Johnson Printing Company, 1994.

Sandoz, Mari. *Crazy Horse, Strange Man of the Oglalas.* University of Nebraska Press, 1942.

Turchen, Lesta Van Der Wert. *The Black Hills Expedition of 1875,* 1975.

Van Bruggen, Theodore. *Wildflowers, Grasses, and Other Plants of the Northern Plains and Black Hills.* Interior, So. Dak.: Badlands Natural History Association, 1992.

The following titles are a small sampling of those that may be ordered from the Black Hills Parks & Forests Association, Route 1, Box 190, WCNP, Hot Springs, SD 57747:

Where the Buffalo Roam
Wind Cave–An Ancient World Beneath the Hills
Custer State Park Grasslands
Birdwatcher's Guide to the Black Hills
Devils Tower
Crazy Horse

ABOUT THE AUTHORS

Bert and Jane Gildart share an enthusiasm for adventure, hiking, photography, and natural history.

Bert is a member of the Outdoor Writers Association of America and has been writing about the outdoors for the past twenty years. He has served as a backcountry ranger in Glacier National Park and has written more than three hundred published magazine articles and nine books.

Together, Bert and Jane have hiked hundreds of miles through America's northwest wilderness areas. They spent many months in the Black Hills and collaborated on this hiking guide. They live near Bigfork, Montana.

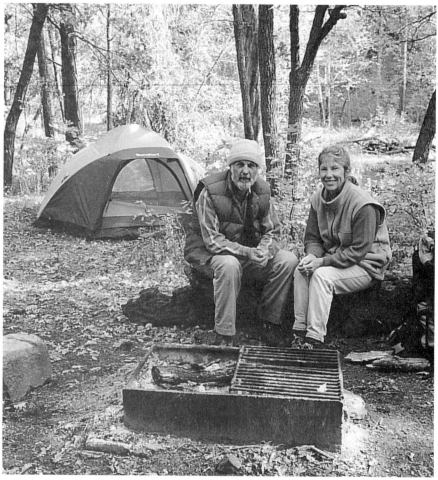

The authors, Bert and Jane Gildart.